BASEBALL SKILLS FOR KIDS

Essential Skills, Drills, and Tips to Play Like a Pro!

JACK RYDELL

Copyright 2024.

SPOTLIGHT MEDIA

ISBN: 978-1-951806-59-0

For questions, please reach out to:

Support@ActivityWizo.com

All Rights Reserved.

No part of this book may be reproduced or transmitted in any form or by any means, electronic or mechanical, including photocopying, recording, or by any other form without written permission from the publisher.

FREE BOOK

SCAN TO GET OUR NEXT BOOK FOR FREE

TABLE OF CONTENTS

INTRODUCTION 1
    CHAPTER OVERVIEW: A SNEAK PEEK AT THE BOOK 3
CHAPTER ONE: BASEBALL 101 7
    THE IMPORTANCE OF LEARNING BASEBALL SKILLS 9
    YOU'RE NEVER TOO YOUNG TO START! 10
    SAFETY TIPS FOR PLAYING BASEBALL 11
    TEAMWORK AND SPORTSMANSHIP 14
CHAPTER TWO: BASIC EQUIPMENT AND GEAR 15
    BATTERS 16
    CATCHERS 18
    TRAINING 19
    MISCELLANEOUS 20
    CHOOSING THE RIGHT BAT AND GLOVE 22
    WEARING A BASEBALL UNIFORM 23
    THE IMPORTANCE OF PROTECTIVE GEAR 23
    CARING FOR EQUIPMENT 24
    PACKING YOUR BASEBALL BAG 26
CHAPTER THREE: WARM-UPS AND CONDITIONING 29
    SIMPLE WARM-UP EXERCISES 31
    STRETCHING ROUTINES 33
    BASIC CONDITIONING EXERCISES 36
    COOL-DOWN EXERCISES 39
    STAYING HYDRATED AND HEALTHY 40
CHAPTER FOUR: BATTING SKILLS 41
    PROPER BATTING STANCE AND GRIP 42

SWING MECHANICS AND FOLLOW-THROUGH 43
IMPROVING HAND-EYE COORDINATION......................... 43
DRILLS TO PRACTICE HITTING 44
ONE-HANDED DRILLS... 46
STRATEGIES FOR FACING DIFFERENT TYPES OF PITCHES 47
PITCH RECOGNITION EXERCISES.. 50

CHAPTER FIVE: FIELDING SKILLS... 51
BASICS OF FIELDING GROUND AND FLY BALLS................ 52
TECHNIQUES FOR CATCHING AND THROWING............. 54
INFIELD VS. OUTFIELD FIELDING SKILLS 57
DRILLS FOR IMPROVING FIELD ACCURACY 58
COMMUNICATING WITH TEAMMATES ON THE FIELD.. 60

CHAPTER SIX: THROWING AND PITCHING 63
PROPER THROWING MECHANICS 64
BASIC PITCHING TECHNIQUES... 65
IMPROVING THROWING ACCURACY AND STRENGTH . 68
INTRO TO ADVANCED PITCHING TECHNIQUES 70

CHAPTER SEVEN: BASERUNNING SKILLS 73
LEADING OFF AND STEALING BASES................................... 74
READING PITCHERS AND FIELDERS 77
IMPROVING BASERUNNING SPEED AND AGILITY........... 80

CHAPTER EIGHT: PLAYING DIFFERENT POSITIONS 83
PITCHER.. 84
CATCHER.. 85
FIRST BASEMAN 85
SECOND BASEMAN 86

THIRD BASEMAN 86
SHORTSTOP... 86
LEFT FIELDER 87
CENTER FIELDER.. 87
RIGHT FIELDER... 88
TRANSITIONING BETWEEN POSITIONS 88
DRILLS FOR EACH POSITION 89
VERSATILITY AND FLEXIBILITY 91
FINDING THE BEST POSITION FOR YOU 92
CHAPTER NINE: GAME STRATEGIES AND TACTICS 93
OBSERVE THE PITCH LIMIT 94
THE CIVILIZED CALL/ 15-RUN RULE 96
DEFENSIVE STRATEGIES... 98
COMMUNICATION AND TEAMWORK....................... 100
HANDLING HIGH-PRESSURE SITUATIONS 101
DEVELOPING A GAME PLAN 102
CHAPTER TEN: PRACTICING AND IMPROVING 103
SETTING GOALS FOR IMPROVEMENT...................... 104
CREATING A PRACTICE SCHEDULE 106
PLAYING TO YOUR STRENGTHS AND WEAKNESSES 107
CREATE AN EXERCISE ROUTINE................................ 108
TURN MISTAKES INTO LESSONS............................... 109
TIPS FOR STAYING MOTIVATED 110
CHAPTER ELEVEN: MENTAL TOUGHNESS 113
TECHNIQUES FOR PERFORMANCE ANXIETY................... 114
CHAPTER TWELVE: PLAYING WITH RESPECT AND SPORTSMANSHIP 119

    HANDLING WINS AND LOSSES GRACEFULLY 121

    BUILDING TEAM SPIRIT 122

    LIFELONG BENEFITS OF PLAYING WITH INTEGRITY 122

CHAPTER THIRTEEN: BEYOND THE BASICS 125

    UPGRADING YOUR PASSING THROW 126

    ADVANCED HITTING TIP 127

    ADVANCED PITCHING 127

    TIPS, EQUIPMENT, DRILLS, AND RESOURCES 128

    STORIES AND TIPS FROM PRO PLAYERS 130

CONCLUSION 133

INTRODUCTION

So, you're thinking about playing a little baseball? Well, we've got good news for you: You've come to the right place! In this book, we've put together a collection of drills, practice tips, and stories that will help you build your skills and take your game to the next level.

Not interested yet? Well, here's just a taste of some of the many amazing things you'll experience inside this book as we explore the inner world of Baseball Skills for Kids together:

- Tips to get yourself into better hand/eye coordination at bat
- How to deal with curveballs, sliders, and screwballs
- Strategies for fielding grounders and catching fly balls
- Pitching grips for changeups, curveballs, and more
- Tips for stealing bases and nailing perfect slides
- How to read pitchers and fielders like Ty Cobbs
- Where to find free equipment if your team needs it
- Inspiring stories like the tale of Mordecai Brown, a 3-fingered pitcher with a 14-year career.

That's just a little of what you can expect inside, but there's much, much more. Starting off with a quick crash course in baseball history, we'll quickly move into some basics, like the equipment you'll need, and proper warm-up and cool-down exercises, From there, we'll go into the fundamentals of batting, fielding, and pitching.

It won't all be basic — we've got a little something for everyone — so we'll also cover stealing bases, playing different positions, and the nitty gritty of communication tips, game strategies, and tactics you can learn and adapt to make your own.

After that, we'll turn our shared focus onto practice. You're going to be doing a lot of it, so we'll cover drills that you can use to form a solid foundation that you can build on into the future.

Finally, we'll go over tips to keep your cool, cover things like good sportsmanship that baseball can teach you, and finish up with some inspiring stories from real pro players. This book also contains a special introduction to advanced techniques, including free resources you can use.

CHAPTER OVERVIEW: A SNEAK PEEK AT THE BOOK

Before we get started, we'll give you a sneak peek into the wide range of tips, techniques, exercises, and strategies that await you inside this book.

Chapter One: Baseball 101 – We'll cover a brief history of baseball and some of the skills this game will teach you, but we'll also talk about the perks of playing baseball for younger players and discuss safety tips, proper sportsmanship, and the importance of teamwork.

Chapter Two: Basic Equipment and Gear – You've got to have the right gear, and in Chapter Two, we'll tell you exactly what gear you need to get started and how to pick your equipment with confidence. Along the way, we'll cover the right way to wear a baseball uniform, the importance of protective gear, and how to take care of that fancy new equipment. If all that equipment seems like a lot to lug around, don't worry — we'll finish the chapter by telling you how to pack it all up in your baseball bag.

Chapter Three: Warmup and Conditioning: Warming up helps you make sure you're playing at your best and helps prevent injuries you might not notice until you get home. We'll cover some simple warm-up and stretching routines and conditioning exercises to sharpen your game, then close the chapter with hydration and nutrition tips, plus cool-down exercises to use before you go home.

Chapter Four: Batting Skills: Batting isn't just swinging at the ball; it's a matter of proper stance, positioning, grip, and swing-through mechanics. We'll explore what you need to know about batting and give you some tips to improve your hand-eye coordination, along with practice drills and a few different strategies for dealing with various types of pitches.

Chapter Five: Fielding Skills: This chapter will teach you the right way to field fly balls and grounders. We'll also cover proper stance and glove positioning, followed by a comparison of infield and outfield skills, so you can create your own useful strategies. Accuracy drills will come after that, and we'll discuss communicating with your teammates on the field to ensure that everyone's on the same page.

Chapter Six: Throwing and Pitching: Techniques, grips, and proper throwing mechanics will be explored in this chapter, and we'll go over some vital safety tips to help you avoid arm injury. These will come in handy while you're practicing the strength and accuracy drills we'll include here, followed by a brief introduction to advanced pitching techniques.

Chapter Seven: Baserunning Skills: In this chapter we'll go over baserunning basics, stealing, leading off, and everyone's favorite—sliding safely into the base! Next, we'll cover how to read fielders and the pitcher. Then we'll throw in some speed and agility drills to further sharpen your skills. Finally, we'll give you some time-tested strategies for effective baserunning that you can put to good use.

Chapter Eight: Playing Different Positions: This chapter talks about the nine different field positions; you'll learn what each is supposed to do and which skills they require. We'll also share advice on switching positions and how this will give you the flexibility that can make a good baseball player into a great one. Before moving on, we'll close the chapter with some tips on how to find the best position for you.

Chapter Nine: Game Strategies and Tactics: An important key to winning is understanding the rules of baseball and having a few basic offensive and defensive strategies that you can put into play. We'll cover this, along with some tips that can help you make lightning-fast decisions and talk about the communication and teamwork your team is going to need. We'll end this chapter with advice about how to deal with pressure when the game is on and working out a game plan with your coach.

Chapter Ten: Practicing and Improving: In this chapter, we'll tell you why you should love practice and how you can set goals to become the player you want to be. This includes setting up a schedule that you can stick to, identifying your weaknesses and strengths, and learning from your mistakes. We'll end the chapter with some motivation tips to keep you going and remind you that, above all, baseball should be fun!

Chapter Eleven: Mental Toughness: Developing mental toughness will help to make sure you stay focused, and in this chapter, you'll learn a game plan for doing just that. We'll tell you how to concentrate when you're stressed and how to cope with setbacks or game-plan mistakes. Next, we'll talk about how to build confidence in your growing baseball skills and ways to mentally rehearse your games. Finally, we'll cover relaxation tips and how the right attitude will make sure that your game is always getting better.

Chapter Twelve: Playing with Respect and Sportsmanship: Everyone knows how to win, but do you know the proper way to lose? You'll need to! Baseball is all about respect — for your coaches, opponents, and teammates — and that respect needs to be maintained even when you don't all get along. Learning this now can transform you into a positive role model, and you'll discover that the benefits of this attitude will be valuable throughout the rest of your life — so be sure not to skip this chapter.

Chapter Thirteen: Beyond the Basics: In our final chapter, we'll introduce you to some advanced baseball skills and share some resources so you can find more tips and tricks to keep improving your game after finishing this book. We'll also relate some inspiring stories from pro baseball players that describe how baseball can help develop good character and skills that will take you far in life.

Now that we've gotten your attention, find a comfy spot, and let's enter the *Baseball Skills for Kids* stadium together.

It's time to play ball!

CHAPTER ONE: BASEBALL 101

They say that baseball is "as American as apple pie," and in a way, that's true. However, the sport that we know and love today is descended from the bat and ball games of many different cultures. For instance, the oldest version comes from ancient Egypt (around 2500 B.C.) in the form of a game called *seker-hemat*. The name means simply "batting the ball."

Pharaohs used to play *seker-hemat* with their high priests, but aside from hitting a ball, it didn't resemble modern baseball much at all. Across the world in Mesoamerica, there were games like *juego de pelota maya* — the Mayan Ballgame — which were played with heavy rubber balls that were kept moving on the court using the forearms, rackets, hand-stones, or bats.

Baseball as we know it today, however, likely derived in the 1800s from the British games of rounders, cricket, and town ball, but wouldn't become the game that we're used to until around 1845. At that time, Knickerbocker Base Ball Club members William H. Tucker and William R. Wheaton created the Knickerbocker Rules and the first organized baseball team — the New York Knickerbockers, also known as the Knickerbocker Nine.

The Knickerbocker Rules added bases, set 90 feet apart, and dictated that three outs were allowed per team each inning. Pitching was also a little different — only underhanded throws were allowed (like throwing a horseshoe) — but by 1884, overhand pitching was permitted, and in 1889, the "four balls, three strikes" standard came into play.

Oddly enough, it took until 1959 before the standardization of ballpark playing fields' dimensions and design. Before that, players often met on repurposed polo fields or any available parks they could find, where they were at the mercy of the weather and terrain.

Through a combination of ballpark standards and the evolution of its rules since the 1845 New York Knickerbockers first laid their foundations, modern baseball in America finally emerged.

It took a long time, but when you consider that over 100 nations around the world now play what is known as "America's favorite pastime," it's safe to say that the New York Knickerbockers were definitely on to something!

Don't take our word for it, though.

Once you've played a few innings of baseball, you will understand for yourself. There's something about the crack of the ball against the bat, stealing those bases, hitting your first home run, and the good times that you'll have working together with your new best friends—your teammates.

THE IMPORTANCE OF LEARNING BASEBALL SKILLS

Aside from being fun, baseball can teach you skills that you will carry with you for the rest of your life. Here are just a few life lessons that America's pastime can teach you:

Social Skills and Teamwork: With proper communication, a team becomes a powerful force of nature, capable of doing much more than any individual team member could do on their own. Baseball can teach you this important life lesson early, and once you know the power of a team, the sky's the limit!

Patience Under Pressure: Baseball teaches you to have patience under pressure. Batters know that it's not easy to keep your eye on the ball when people are watching, and even harder to let it whiz by when you know it's going to be a foul. Infielders must guard bases against steals and opposing batters. In the outfield, you must position yourself just right to catch a rapidly descending ball and know exactly where to throw it next. It's all about patience, planning, and performing under pressure.

Learning From Victory and Defeat: Both victory and defeat teach players sportsmanship, and you can learn from both. If you win the game, identify the winning strategies your team used to help you win against others in future games. If you lose the game, try to identify what strategies the other team used to learn how to counter them. Win or lose, there are lessons to be learned, and this is another important aspect of life.

Strength and Agility: Baseball is a good workout for both the upper and lower body. Strength is required to hit a home run, for instance, and you won't steal many bases if you don't train to be quick.

Solid Work Ethic: By playing baseball and setting training goals, you'll quickly get firsthand experience in a very important principle: With hard work, you can accomplish anything. As long as you learn from your victories and mistakes, you'll always have a solid plan for what you'll need to work on to win.

YOU'RE NEVER TOO YOUNG TO START!

Some kids start playing baseball as early as five years old, but any time is a good time to start. Just be sure to enjoy yourself, and keep in mind that it takes time to learn to play well.

Baseball legends Barry Bonds and Ty Cobb both started playing early, just like you're about to do, but they didn't develop their amazing skills magically or overnight—they learned and developed over years of practice.

For now, make your goals simple: Focus on having fun, and see what baseball can teach you. Try different positions until you find one that's perfect for you. After that, challenge yourself to learn a different position. Get to know your team and see what you can learn from each other — on and off the field.

With a little hard work and a whole lot of fun, you'll be amazed at how quickly your personal game improves and how formidable your team can become. You've just got to put in the practice!

SAFETY TIPS FOR PLAYING BASEBALL

While we'll share some more detailed safety advice as we move along, there are a few basic, foundational rules that you'll want to observe at all times. To keep things simple, we'll divide them into three categories:

- Safety Gear
- Play
- Practice

Safety Gear

Catchers: A catcher needs to be properly armored any time they will be handling the ball — whether it's in practice, play, or even goofing off in the bullpen. This means wearing a throat guard, face mask, and helmet, along with an athletic supporter and protective cup, if applicable. Catchers also need a full-length chest protector, shin guards, and a catcher's mitt to always ensure their safety.

Batters: A batting helmet is always worn when they're waiting to play, at play, or running the bases. These helmets need to fit each individual player well, and they should be in good condition. Damaged helmets should be replaced immediately and not used, and if the helmet has a chin strap, it should be secured when the helmet is worn.

Sliding Shorts: These are special undergarments with extra hip padding, worn underneath the uniform pants to allow a player to slide more easily. While sliding shorts are optional, they're highly recommended for practice sessions and confident sliding during games.

Baseball Cleats: For baseball, it's important to stick with plastic spikes rather than metal ones.

Male Players: It's important to protect your sensitive areas with an athletic supporter and cup.

Other Optional Gear: batting gloves, shin and foot guards, and mouth guards. While you can play without them, it's safer to at least practice with this gear first to help avoid injury while you're still learning the game. We'll go over equipment in depth in Chapter Two.

Play

Always have a first aid kit and a working cell phone ready for emergencies.

Never play or practice without adult supervision. If your coach is not present, then a parent, legal guardian, or other trusted adult should be there to make sure everyone stays safe.

The field should be clean before play, so if you're using a local public park, give it a good cleanup first, and again before you leave. Always leave the field better than it was when you got there.

Use breakaway bases instead of fixed ones. These bases snap onto a rubber mat, so you have a base that can move when a player slides in. To reduce the chance of injury during slides, breakaway bases are definitely something you'll want to have.

Make sure you have plenty of water and/or sports drinks to stay hydrated; keep in mind that some sports drinks contain unnecessary amounts of sugar, sodium, and calories, so water is generally the better choice. Additionally, snacks for extra energy are always a good idea—granola, fruits, and small sandwiches are all excellent options for snacks on the go.

Practice

Get into the habit of stretching before practice and games to get your body warmed up and ready. It only takes a few minutes, but it prepares your muscles for exertion and reduces the chance of soreness and sprains.

Pitching is hard on the arms and shoulders, and rotating pitchers at regular intervals not only gives more kids a chance to pitch but also helps prevent injury. The American Sports Medicine Institute recommends that pitchers aged 7-8 years should only throw 50 pitches a day, and no more than 75 per week, but you should consult your league rules for their specific regulations. Nine- and ten-year-old players shouldn't throw more than 75 pitches per day and 100 per week. Those ages 10-12 may pitch 85 times per day, but no more than 115 pitches per week. Any arm pain felt during pitching should be respected—no more pitching until the pain goes away, period!

Pitchers also need to rest their pitching arms for three consecutive months every year. During this time, overhead arm activity should be avoided. That means no tennis, volleyball, water polo, or aggressive swimming—though light swimming is okay.

TEAMWORK AND SPORTSMANSHIP

We can't stress one thing enough: Good sportsmanship and teamwork are the hallmarks of all great baseball players.

When you win a game, you shouldn't gloat or be mean about it. A "good sport" is gracious about winning, thanking the other team, and complimenting them on good plays or strategies they noticed during the game. It's good sportsmanship, and besides, why waste time gloating when you could be writing down the strategies that helped you win this time?

Don't be a "bad sport" when you lose, either. Accusing other players of cheating or talking down to them won't do anything but make your own team look bad. Instead, you can shake hands or say things like "We'll get you next time!" It's good sportsmanship, but also practical—a smart baseball player knows that defeat is just another lesson in how to play better next time.

By examining what the other team did and didn't do, defeat can work in your favor, because you can set practice goals to help make sure that you're ready for them next time.

In fact, this is something that the entire team needs to get in the habit of doing. When your team communicates with each other and pays attention to strategies on the diamond that work, you can also learn these tricks and make them your own.

In a nutshell, have fun, be gracious—whether you win or lose—and remember that teamwork and communication win games. There's no "I" in team, as they say, and when everyone works together, you'll be a baseball force to be reckoned with!

In the next chapter, we'll cover the gear you need to play baseball as well as how to care for and pack them.

CHAPTER TWO:
BASIC EQUIPMENT AND GEAR

When you're getting started, you'll want to make sure that you've got the right gear from the get-go. We'll cover the basics of your essential gear below, listing them first, then giving a quick explanation for each so you'll know how they function and why they're so important.

BATTERS

While you can scoot by on casual or pickup baseball games with just a helmet and a bat, there's more gear to consider. Here's what you ideally need:

- Baseball bat
- Batting helmet
- Cleats
- Batting gloves
- Fielder's gloves
- Guards (elbow, leg, foot, and mouth)
- Protective cup, if applicable

Baseball Bat

You can't do much batting without owning an actual bat, so this is a must. While you could go with a wooden bat, metal bats are usually much lighter and easier to use for longer periods of time. Also, make sure that the bat you choose conforms with what your local Little League requires if you're playing for a local team. We'll talk more about choosing the perfect bat later in this chapter.

Batting Helmet

Each player needs their own batting helmet. While helmets that include face or jaw guards are optional, it's a good idea to go with them for added safety. Baseballs fly pretty fast, so if you get hit with one, you'll be glad for that face or jaw guard. However, it's important to make sure the mask or jaw guard comes pre-installed in the helmet—any guard that you have to put in yourself won't be as reliable.

Cleats

Ever tried running bases without cleats? Cleats help to provide a grip on terrain which allows you to run the bases and turn sharply without slipping. You'll need to go with rubber or plastic cleats; Metal is not recommended when you're getting started and is not allowed in most youth leagues.

Batting Gloves

While these are technically optional, batting gloves make baseball safer by improving grip and absorbing some of the force when you swing a fantastic hit.

Fielder's Gloves

When not at bat, you'll need infield or outfield gloves to ensure that you can catch the ball and move it quickly when you need to. Here's a quick explanation of the seven different glove types and what they do:

Catcher's Mitt: Clam-shaped and larger than other gloves, catcher's mitts have extra padding and wide webbing so fast-flying balls may be caught safely and easily.

First Base Glove: First base gloves are large, curved, and don't have individual finger spacing, so they're good for throws, and balls may be caught or easily scooped up.

Second Base Glove: Second base gloves are designed so the ball may be caught and immediately thrown wherever it's needed. To accomplish this, they're made to be lighter than other gloves and have a shallower pocket, so the ball doesn't get stuck at the worst possible time.

Third Base Glove: Deep-pocketed, long, and wide, third base gloves are designed to catch the fast-moving balls that tend to rocket towards third base.

Shortstop Glove: Shortstops need the dexterity of a second base glove but with a longer design for harder-to-catch balls. As a result, you can get away with using one of these for both second base and shortstop positions.

Pitcher's Glove: You'll find a wide variety of pitcher's gloves, but the main concern is usually the webbing in the glove, as it can help to conceal the ball until the pitcher puts it into play.

Outfield Glove: Longer than other gloves and with a deep pocket, outfield gloves allow you to jump and still catch the ball if you manage to reach it!

Guards (Elbow, Leg, Foot, and Mouth)

Guards provide extra protection from fast-flying baseballs and come in many varieties that cover the elbows, ankles or legs, and even the feet. Mouthguards should definitely be used, especially when batting.

Protective Cup

A protective cup is a standard part of the protection gear that's required for all male players in local leagues.

CATCHERS

Catchers need to be well-armored in order to properly deal with those fast-moving pitches. Below is a list of gear that every catcher needs:

- Catcher's mitt
- Catcher's helmet/mask (with a throat guard)
- Chest protector

- Leg guards

Catcher's Mitt

As explained in the glove section of baseball gear, catcher's mitts are larger than others, clam-shaped, and packed with the extra padding you need to intercept fastballs.

Catcher's Helmet/Mask (with Throat Guard)

The catcher's helmet should include a mask and throat guard—and this is non-negotiable. You never know where a pitch might end up, so this extra protection is vital for the catcher's position.

Chest Protector

A full-length chest protector uses thick padding to protect the catcher as fully as possible behind the plate.

Leg Guards

Without leg guards, the knees and shins are vulnerable to heavy, fast-flying baseballs. Needless to say, these are a vital part of the whole package.

You can typically purchase a helmet, chest protector, and leg guards in one bundle—just look for catcher's gear sets to get it all in one go.

TRAINING

There are several items that can really ramp up your baseball training and help you learn the game faster. Here are some examples:

- Weighted training baseballs (optional)
- Extra baseballs
- Hitting net

- Batting tees
- Breakaway bases

Weighted Training Baseballs (Optional)

Weighted baseballs are great for pitcher training, but not something you'll need right away. When you've gotten used to pitching and playing with regular baseballs, these can help you build muscle so you can get to the next level.

Extra Baseballs

You're going to lose a lot of baseballs, and that's unavoidable, so be sure that you have extra ones ready. It'd be a shame to have to stop a game just because you ran out of balls!

Hitting Net

Hitting nets allows you to practice swings with confidence without a catcher squatting behind you. These are great for practice and tend to be quite portable, so you can bring them to parks or other places where you'd like to get in a little practice.

Batting Tees

Batting tees give you the power to suspend a ball so you can practice hitting when a pitcher is unavailable.

Breakaway Bases

Breakaway bases help you make practice diamonds anywhere you like, and since they aren't fixed to the ground, but rather on rubber mats, they're also safer to practice sliding with.

MISCELLANEOUS

In this section, we're listing several miscellaneous items, some of which are important and others that are optional. Let's take a look!

- First aid kit
- Wrist braces and athletic tape
- Baseball bag
- Sliding shorts
- Portable water cooler
- Uniforms

First Aid Kit

A first aid kit is required for playing baseball—or any other sport, for that matter. Be sure that you have one on hand in case of emergency.

Wrist Braces and Athletic Tape

Your wrists are one of the weakest parts of your arm, so many baseball players tape their wrists with athletic tape or use braces to reinforce them. This helps to prevent sprains and muscle cramps, and it adds strength and stability when you're at bat or catching pitches.

Baseball Bag

You'll need something to carry your gear in, so a baseball bag is a must. While any large bag will do, sporting goods suppliers have specialized baseball bags, with useful features like separate storage for your cleats.

Sliding Shorts

Sliding shorts give your hips a little extra padding for added protection when you're sliding into a base.

Portable Water Cooler

Staying hydrated during practice and games is important, and investing in a portable water cooler now is a great way to save money on bottled water later, as well as reduce waste from discarded plastic.

Uniforms

Regular pants and shirts are okay for now, but eventually, you'll need a uniform. You can have them made at any number of places but check with your parent or guardian first—if one has sewing talents, they may be able to help with uniforms, and local businesses sometimes even sponsor teams in their area to help with the cost of uniforms and gear.

CHOOSING THE RIGHT BAT AND GLOVE

Picking out the right bat and glove is much easier than you might think. Starting with the bat, look for a length between 27 and 42 inches. To figure out what length you need, put your cleats on and then stand up the bat on the floor next to you. The bat should reach right up to your hip—anything higher than that means that the bat will be too long to use effectively. For younger children, start with a 26-inch bat for a child that is 3 feet 5 inches tall, and for every 4–5 inches they grow, add another inch to the bat length to calculate the best size.

After determining the right length for your bat, it's just a matter of choosing a comfortable weight and the width of the barrel. For weight, lighter bats give you more speed and control, while heavier ones hit with more power. The barrel of a bat is measured at its widest part, and for most youth-league players, these widths generally range from 2 ¼ to 2 ⅝ inches.

Now that you've got a bat picked out, you'll need to pick a glove. Don't worry, because this isn't very difficult, either! The key is to go a little bigger than you think you'll need. For kids ages 4–5, 10- to 10 ½-inch gloves are ideal, while an 8-year-old player should use an 11-inch glove. Usually, 11 ½ to 12 ½ inches is the perfect size for adults.

WEARING A BASEBALL UNIFORM

When you see baseball on TV, those snappy uniforms really seem to shine. The good news is that it's pretty easy to make sure your whole team is looking sharp with just a few simple rules:

Team caps should have a slightly curved brim and are worn facing forward at all times—except the catcher, who needs to wear theirs backward so their masks will fit.

Jerseys are tucked in, and if the uniforms come with belts, wear them to keep your pants up with the tucked jersey in place.

If players are wearing sleeves under their jerseys, everyone should have the same color. Cleat colors should match as well—the brand doesn't matter, but the colors should match.

Shoes should be fully laced, with laces of the same color as the rest of the team is wearing.

Finally, it's good to wear uniforms to practice. It looks sharp, but more importantly, you need to get used to wearing the outfits, so they don't become a distraction during a game.

THE IMPORTANCE OF PROTECTIVE GEAR

While we've talked about protective gear, this subject is important enough to warrant a little emphasis. Safety gear is important, and you should not play baseball without it. Helmets protect the batter's head from fast-moving balls, and jaw or mouth guards do the same. Without them, serious injuries can occur.

In addition, catchers need to have chest, face, and leg protection, and every male player needs to wear an athletic cup—after all, that's one place you definitely don't want to get hit with a baseball!

"Safety first" is always the best policy, so if you don't have protective gear, don't play until you do—it's as simple as that.

CARING FOR EQUIPMENT

Baseball gear can last a long time, provided you take care of it. In this section, we'll give you some cleaning basics to help you get into good habits when it comes to your gear. One note: If the equipment you selected came with special instructions, follow those! These are just some best practices that you can use for now to maintain your gear.

Baseball Bats

If you're using a wooden bat, make sure you dry it quickly whenever it gets wet, as wood can easily warp if you don't. You'll also want to wipe your bat down with a little rubbing alcohol on a clean rag to avoid a buildup of bacteria.

Metal bats are much easier to maintain—just wipe them clean, dry them off, and store them away!

Baseball Gloves

With baseball gloves, you want to be a little more careful, since they're made of leather. Start the cleaning process by rubbing off dirt with a dry and clean cloth. What you can't get with that, you should rub off with a little leather cleaner and a soft rag.

Once you've gotten the dirt off, make sure that the glove is dry before storing it away. Every other week, apply a little glove conditioning oil—just make sure it's approved for your brand of glove.

Finally, a little disinfectant sprayed inside the glove can help keep it from getting moldy or stinky, so be sure to do this at least once a month, though every two weeks is better!

Catcher's Gear

Catcher's gear usually comes with some cleaning instructions, but generally, what you need to do is wipe your gear down thoroughly after every use. After that, let it air out in the open for a few hours before you store it in a cool, dry place.

Before the next time you play, check to make sure that all straps and hooks are in good shape. You should also inspect your helmet and face mask for cracks. If you find any cracks, replace your equipment. Head injuries can cause permanent brain damage, or worse. It is very important to invest in a new one before playing again, as repairs and patch jobs won't hold up. You should always prioritize replacing protective gear whenever it becomes damaged.

Cleats

Cleats can get pretty gunky, so you'll want to have a stiff brush ready and a little bit of dish soap for cleaning them. Start by taking your cleats outside and smacking them together to loosen any mud or trapped dirt.

After that, give them a good soak in warm water for about five minutes, then start going at them with your scrub brush. Once that's done, a soft rag, a little water, and some dish soap will help you with the last of the cleaning. When you're satisfied that they're clean, give them a rinse with the water hose. Once you dry your cleats, they are ready to put them away.

PACKING YOUR BASEBALL BAG

Packing your baseball bag properly takes a little practice, but before you know it, you'll be able to stow away your gear quickly. The best way to learn is to lay out the gear you need, putting items of similar size next to each other. That way, you'll have a good idea of what will fit in the various pockets and compartments of the bag you've chosen.

Cleats usually have their own compartment, and you can roll uniforms up, so they won't wrinkle or take up as much space. You can also roll up and tuck your batting gloves just about anywhere. However, catching gloves requires careful placement because you don't want to accidentally flatten them!

An example of what to pack might look like this:

- Uniform
- Mitts and gloves
- Protection gear
- Cleats
- Small personal items

There is usually a sleeve for your bat, as well. As far as water and snacks go, it might be a good idea to keep those somewhere separate—that way, you won't have to worry about them accidentally spilling on your equipment.

Last but not least, if you've chosen a baseball bag with straps, these are a great way to carry your helmet or other protective gear on the outside of your bag, where it's less likely to receive damage. If you don't have straps, it's fine to keep these items in your bag. You can pad them with clothing but make enough space to help ensure they don't get squashed and potentially damaged.

Now that we've discussed the gear you need and how to care for it, let's move on to learning about the importance of warm-ups and conditioning.

CHAPTER THREE: WARM-UPS AND CONDITIONING

We cannot stress enough the importance of warming up before playing or practicing. With a few warm-up exercises to get your heart pumping and circulating through your muscles, you'll be off to a good start.

Stretches come next, which help you gain flexibility and prepare your muscles for fast responses while you play or practice. Then, move on to conditioning exercises, working out core muscles and the upper and lower body to condition them for pitching, hitting, and fielding.

At this point, you're ready for practice or play—but you're not quite done.

After the game, some cool-down exercises help get your blood pressure and heart back to a slower, more relaxed rate. A final round of stretches helps loosen up taut muscles and encourages healthy blood flow to nourish the tissue.

Timewise, you'll want to start with 5-10 minutes of warm-up exercises, followed by about 10 minutes of stretching, then 10-20 minutes of conditioning exercises. When the game is over, do 5-10 minutes of cool-down exercises and another 5-10 minutes of stretching to complete your routine.

Further down, we'll provide some example exercises to help you put together your routines. Feel free to add or remove exercises as you like—these are just to give you a starting point to work with.

If you feel your routine is getting dull or simply want to mix things up, then by all means, expand your routine! Just be sure to group it into the same order—warmup, stretches, conditioning, and cool-down before your final stretching session.

If you stick with this, you'll reduce your chances of injury, and over time, you'll see firsthand the difference that this simple routine can really make in your game.

With that said, you'll need those exercises, so let's get moving!

SIMPLE WARM-UP EXERCISES

Below, you'll find a sampling of some simple warm-up exercises that you can use to build your warm-up routine. We'll describe each one. Keep in mind that, while your target is 5–10 minutes, a little longer is fine. Just try not to go over 15 minutes until you've gotten used to warm-up exercises—the last thing you need is a muscle cramp that keeps you from practice or play!

Standing Knee Hugs

Standing knee hugs are great warm-up exercises. They stretch and strengthen the lower back, hamstrings, and hips. As a bonus, they help you to develop good balance, and over time, you'll find that this makes an enormous difference in your game.

Here's how you do a standing knee hug:

1. Stand up straight with your feet shoulder-width apart.
2. Pull your left knee up as close as you can get it to your chest.
3. Try to hold this for 10–20 seconds.
4. Slowly lower and release your leg, maintaining your posture as straight as you can. Then, repeat with the right leg.

Starting off, do 8–10 reps with each leg. A week or two later, you can try adding more reps and increasing the hold time until, eventually, you're balancing and holding your knee for about 40 seconds.

Jogging

After your knee hugs, jogging a lap around the playing field is an excellent, low-impact way to get warmed up. Not only does it help you build endurance and stronger legs, but it also helps build stronger bones.

As with the other exercises in this chapter, you can increase the laps as needed but don't forget that we're just warming up here. Too many warm-up exercises before the game will leave you tired, instead of flexible and invigorated—so don't overdo it!

Base Sprints

Setting out your breakaway bases or some rubber cones in a diamond pattern gives you a way to practice sprinting. These short bursts of speed help warm you up for running and stealing bases, as well as get used to your cleats to take those sharp corners.

Sprint to first base, pause a few moments, then move on to second. Keep going, pausing at each base, until you get to home base. One trip around the bases is good to start with and gets you ready for the movements you'll need in the game.

Throwing Practice

Simple throwing practice is always a great way to warm up. If you want to use your breakaway bases, you can have teammates in the infield and outfield and have someone call the base or other position to throw to.

This will be awkward at first, but in time, it teaches you to get the ball where it needs to go quickly, almost without thinking about it. On top of that, the more you do this with your team, the better you'll work together during a game.

Calling out where the ball is going to go is good practice, but flying baseballs sometimes have a mind of their own—so warming up with this exercise will help give you a taste of that before a game. This also teaches the importance of knowing what areas each player must cover, and the best way to develop a proper defense is to practice.

For warmups, underhand throws are best, so players can get practice hitting and chasing down grounders and other types of hits. There will be more pitching and hitting exercises to come later, so don't worry.

Next, it's time for stretching and conditioning, and then you'll be ready for the actual game!

STRETCHING ROUTINES

After your quick warm-up exercises, some focused upper and lower body stretching is in order. Between pitching, hitting, and running to intercept rapidly descending baseballs, your muscles get a serious workout.

Gentle stretching before a game or practice will get your muscles flexible and ready for what's ahead, and by stretching after the game, you'll get blood flowing to those same muscles and help prevent cramping later.

Upper-Body Stretches

Below, you'll find four upper body stretches, but feel free to add other exercises of your own. These are definitely keepers, though, and are great for forming your first stretching routines.

Arm Circles

Arm circles help warm up and tone your shoulders and arms, and they're easy to do. Here's how to do arm circles:

1. Standing up, hold your arms straight out beside you, palm-up.
2. Move your arms in circles, about one foot wide, for about 10 seconds.
3. Repeat the exercise with your palms down.

1. Do this three times to begin with, and you can add more times as needed.

Finger Flexes

Finger stretches are a great way to prepare yourself for throwing and catching. In time, your fingers will also become stronger and more flexible. Here's how to get there with practice:

1. While standing, hold both arms out directly in front of you, palms up.
2. Stretch your fingers and thumb down as far as you can without discomfort. Repeat this five times.
3. Turning your hands over, repeat the exercise, but stretch your fingers and thumbs up this time.
2. Repeat 1-2 times for now. First, with your palms up, then palms down. It doesn't seem like much, but you'll quickly notice the difference when you go to play.

Shoulder Stretches

You'll use your shoulders a lot playing baseball, so shoulder stretches are going to come in handy. Here is an easy way to loosen up your shoulders:

1. Hold your elbow up next to your head.
2. Pull gently on your elbow to move it behind your head. Not too far, though—just enough that it feels a little tight.
3. Repeat this with your other arm.

Do this 3-5 times for each arm, and your shoulders should be ready!

Torso Twists

Torso twists help to get your core muscles ready for a workout and are the last of our upper body stretches. Here's how to do a standing torso twist:

1. Stand with your legs shoulder-width apart, with your hands on your hips.
2. Leading with your shoulders, keep your feet in place and twist 90 degrees to the right, holding it for a second.
3. Repeat on your left side.

Do this three times on each side for now, and you can add more later after you get used to the exercise.

Lower-Body Stretches

Now that you've done your upper body stretches, we need to stretch your lower body before we move on to conditioning exercises. Below are three examples you can use for your first routine and add to as needed.

Toe Touches

Toe touches work your hamstrings and your abdominal muscles. Here's a simple toe-touch stretch that you can use:

1. Stand straight with your feet hip-width apart.
2. Bend at the waist as you reach down to touch your toes (or as close as you can get). Keep your legs straight and hold for a second or two before straightening back up again.

Repeat this 10 times, and you're done — or you can do another set of 10 after a brief rest.

Standing Quad Stretch

Standing quad stretches are good for your hip flexor muscles and quadriceps, and they also help with balance and flexibility. Here's how they're done:

1. Standing straight, feet hip-width apart, slowly bend your right leg at the knee behind you and hold it up by the ankle with your right hand. Hold this for 5–10 seconds.

2. Repeat with your left leg, holding another 5–10 seconds.

This takes a while to get used to, but you'll quickly learn balance. For now, do this three times for each leg, and as you get used to it, you can increase the holding time in future sessions until you're up to 30 seconds.

Butterfly Stretches

Groin pulls are a common injury in baseball, and butterfly stretches are a great way to avoid them. This is what you do:

1. Sit down on the floor with your legs in front of you, knees bent, and your feet pressed together.
2. Grabbing your ankles and keeping your back straight, use your elbows and push your knees apart so that your legs move closer to the floor. Do this carefully, stopping when you start to feel the stretch.

Do this 4–5 times to start with, and you can do more as you start to get more limber from the practice.

BASIC CONDITIONING EXERCISES

Baseball conditioning exercises are designed to help you hit, run, and throw better. This can be from exercises that simulate these skills, or ones that target associated muscle groups to help with specific skills.

Below are five examples to get you started.

Jumping Jacks

Jumping jacks are a fantastic conditioning exercise, as they're low-impact and work many muscles at the same time. Aside from benefitting your shoulders, core, glutes, and hip flexors, they're also good for your heart and lungs and can increase your metabolism.

Here's how to do jumping jacks properly:
1. Stand straight with your feet together, your toes pointing forward, and your hands down by your sides.
2. Bending your knees slightly, jump lightly and thrust your legs out wide while swinging your arms up and above your head.
3. When your feet land on the ground, reverse the motions so that your legs go back together, and your arms fall back at your sides.

Start with three sets of 10 jumping jacks. As always, you can add more jacks per set as you start getting used to them. You can also learn other types of jumping jacks, such as burpees, to keep things interesting and work out different muscle groups.

Push-Ups

Push-ups are perfect for batters and pitchers, as they strengthen the triceps, shoulders, and chest. A proper push-up looks like this:
1. Start by getting down on all fours. Then, stretch out so that you're balanced on your toes, with your arms straight down, a little wider than shoulder-width. Your elbows should be slightly bent and your back straight.
2. Tighten your abdominal muscles and inhale, lowering yourself down slowly until your elbows are at a 90-degree angle.
3. Push back up on your hands, and use your chest muscles, exhaling as you do.

Try starting with 5–10 push-ups in a row, then rest for a moment and repeat. As you get used to it, you'll be able to do more push-ups in a row, and eventually, you'll want to do this three times with a quick rest in between each. Don't worry if you can't do many at first—you'll be surprised how many you can do once you get in the habit of doing them every week!

Planks

Planks work out the core muscles at the center of your body, so they're an excellent workout for baseball players to become stronger and increase endurance. This is how a plank is done:

1. Get down in a push-up position, but instead of supporting yourself on your hands, bend your elbows and put your fists forward so that you're supporting your weight on your forearms.
2. Straighten your body out like a board (or plank) and hold this position—you'll feel a tightening in your abs if you're doing it right.
3. Hold for 20 seconds if you can, and then you can relax.

Repeat this three times, and in future sessions, you can try adding another 5-10 seconds as your core muscles get stronger over time. This exercise will be hard at first, so don't give up if you don't make it the full 20 seconds the first time—before you know it, you'll be surprised how long you can hold a plank.

Later, you can learn other types of planks as well (such as the side plank) and really upgrade your workouts.

Figure-8 Drills

Figure-8 drills are a great way to prepare for running bases, and they're easy to set up. You'll need markers—they could be bases, cones, or anything flat and easy to see that you can put on the ground. Once you've got markers, this is how you run the drill:

1. Arrange your markers like one baseball diamond above another. This will make the shape of an angular figure-8.
2. Once the figure-8 is set up, run around the outside of your markers, starting from home to first base, then to

second. Then, run to the left of the marker that represents home plate on the top diamond to round past third base on the top diamond, then to second, then down to first. Next, run straight to third base on your first diamond, then back to home.

Just run it once the first time, and have each teammate do the same. Running these figure-8 patterns will get everyone used to moving quickly and taking the sharp turns needed to navigate bases. It's also a good way to condition the muscles you use for running those bases and get you in the right mindset before the game.

5-10-5 Agility Drills

When someone hits a ball into the sky, you're going to need to be fast. 5-10-5 drills can teach you that—and make you good at it. Here's how to do a 5-10-5:

1. Place three flat markers in a straight line on the ground, each 5 yards apart. You can use breakaway bases for this if you like, but anything flat will do.
2. Starting from the middle marker, sprint as fast as you can to the marker to your right and touch it.
3. Immediately sprint to the farthest marker, tapping it when you get there, then sprint back to the center.

This drill teaches you and your teammates how to sprint in quick, calculated ranges, and it comes in handy for teaching everyone to stay close to their positions, while still being able to quickly defend against the other team.

COOL-DOWN EXERCISES

After the game, you'll want to do some cool-down exercises to reduce your heart rate. Afterward, complete a few stretches to help get blood circulating through those sore muscles. These can be any low-impact exercises. For instance, a light jog around the playing field, followed by 5-10 minutes of the stretches we've already shown you is just about perfect.

STAYING HYDRATED AND HEALTHY

Whether you're doing warmups or actually playing the game, it's important to stay hydrated and ensure that you're getting the proper nutrition. Here are a few quick tips to help:

Always keep fluids available, and while sports drinks help replenish your electrolyte and vitamin levels, make sure you are drinking more water. It's also a good idea to choose sugar-free sports drinks as these are healthier for you.

A clean washcloth, soaked in ice water and placed on the back of the neck can lower your body temperature quickly on a hot day. An ice pack wrapped in a dry cloth feels and works even better.

Snacking about an hour before practice or a game is a good idea. Foods with a high water content and carbs are a good idea—smoothies, fruits, and even warm soup in a thermos are all great options. High-protein and high-carb choices are excellent for snacking as well—eggs, cheese, and nuts are good examples.

Know the signs of dehydration and watch for them in yourself and other players. Symptoms include feeling dizzy, weak, lightheaded, or nauseous. If you experience any of these signs or think another player might be dehydrated, tell your coach right away and take a break to rest and drink water.

CHAPTER FOUR: BATTING SKILLS

Building up your batting skills takes time, but with a little practice and a solid foundation of basic skills, then you'll be hitting those pitches like a pro in no time flat.

You've got to crawl before you can walk, though, so let's start things off right with the proper batting stance and grip, and we'll build up steadily from there.

PROPER BATTING STANCE AND GRIP

Every new batter must learn the proper stance and grip in preparation for swinging at their first pitch. It's fundamental, and once you can do it without thinking, you'll have unlocked an entire treasure trove of upgraded moves that you can use in the future.

The best way to determine the correct distance from home plate in the batter's box is to put the tip of your bat on the bottom edge of the plate at a 45-degree angle. Stand exactly behind that, and you're the perfect distance.

Your basic stance should look like this:

- Feet slightly wider than shoulder-width
- Bend a little at your knees and waist
- Eyes forward (on the pitcher)
- Hands near your back shoulder, holding your bat at 45 degrees
- Weight is distributed evenly between both feet

If you're right-handed, your left hand will be gripping your bat at the lowest point, just above the knob, with your right hand above your left. The knuckles on your hand—the ones you use to knock on a door—should line up perfectly, and if they do, then you're gripping the bat correctly.

SWING MECHANICS AND FOLLOW-THROUGH

The mechanics for swinging a bat are a lot like rocking a baby. Your back shoulder goes up while your front shoulder goes down, and you should shift the weight to your hip, rather than to your back foot.

With that loaded hip, lift your front leg and turn into your swing as your front foot goes back down. Keep your eyes forward, and the force from the leg lift and your turning hips—along with your arms swinging the bat, of course—should connect with a crack to the ball, and the game is on!

The coiled-up energy a batter generates is a little hard to describe, but a quick internet search can bring up videos that show the swing in slow motion, and you'll see what we mean. It's all about maintaining your stance, readying your muscles to explode into motion, and delivering all that force into your bat.

When we list drills later in this chapter, pay special attention to the medicine ball drill. This is a way to practice the motions and train your muscle memory in preparation for the perfect swing.

IMPROVING HAND-EYE COORDINATION

While the majority of learning your way around the batter's craft will be through practice, there are a few things you can do to gain better control. Here are a few quick tips for improving your hand-eye coordination:

> **Try using a smaller ball.** Since it's harder to hit, you're going to learn more granular control. Start with a smaller baseball on a tee or have someone toss the ball to you with

a nice, easy underarm throw. Don't forget safety gear—small balls still hurt if they hit you!

Try hitting a smaller ball with a smaller bat—in this case, a broomstick. Get your parents' permission to purchase a broom or mop stick and ask them to help you shorten it so it's about the same length as your bat. After that, underarm throws or a batting tee will give you some practice in well-placed and controlled hits.

Get a second, heavier, bat. For instance, if you're using a lightweight aluminum bat, practice with a wooden one. The extra weight will help beef up your arms a little, improving your strength and endurance, and you'll learn better control along the way. You can also find training bats that work the same way, as well as hitting knobs that attach to your own bat to add weight.

DRILLS TO PRACTICE HITTING

In this section, we've got some drills that can help both new and experienced batters improve their swing power and accuracy.

Medicine Ball Toss

Medicine balls are large, solid balls that you can find at any sporting goods store and most gyms. Tossing these weighted balls is a great drill, especially for younger batters, because it helps teach the powerful movements of the lower half of a proper swing. Here's what you need to do:

1. Holding a medicine ball low and centered in front of you, stand with your legs shoulder-width apart.
2. Step forward with your left leg and bring the medicine ball back like you're about to swing a bat.

3. Continue the motion forward and up, as you would with the swing, stepping forward with your right foot as you do.
4. Bring the ball back and repeat.

When properly done, this exercise helps build the muscles you use to swing, and it also helps develop muscle memory. A few minutes of practice like this will help you learn proper swinging form, and you'll notice the difference when you go to bat.

Tee Time

The baseball tee is a standard learning tool, and for good reason — it works! By telescoping out, the tee holds the ball suspended where you need it, so that you can practice and learn how to execute a perfect swing.

There are lots of examples for different uses online, but below is a basic tee drill that can teach you to hit standard inside, outside, and middle pitches.

This will just be a matter of where you place the tee, so we'll tell you where it goes to practice each of these three types of hits below:

Inside Pitches: Inside pitches are designed to get very close to the batter to make it harder to swing effectively. To practice hitting these, you need to position the tee behind home plate, a few inches in toward you and a few inches to the right (toward the pitcher). This lets you practice falling back to get a proper swing.

Outside Pitches: Outside pitches are designed to end up just along the side of the home plate. To practice drilling for outside pitches, place your batting tee halfway onto the left edge that's closest to the bottom of the home plate. With outside pitches, you need to learn to let the ball come deeper inside your hitting zone. With that in mind, you can move the tee a little to learn how deep it can go and still be hit properly.

Straight Down the Middle Pitches: For pitches that arrive straight down the middle of the home plate, you'll want to place the batting tee halfway onto the bottom edge of the home plate. This should be right where your stomach and front foot will be as you stride into a strong swing.

These drills will get you started, but you get the idea—when you practice your swinging stance and stride, moving the tee around, you'll start to understand intuitively all the places the ball can go and still be effectively hit.

One final note for tees: With younger players, who are still learning to follow through with their swing, you should use a soccer ball or a basketball on the tee. They're much easier to hit, and once the young player gains a bit of confidence and better form, you can switch to a smaller ball.

ONE-HANDED DRILLS

While we don't recommend one-handed drills for the newest players (they can encourage bad form) for more experienced batters looking to learn a little more control, they can be an excellent tool.

When you're batting, the left hand provides power, while the right-hand guides the bat. These drills help strengthen the arms, and as a result, you'll get a faster and more powerful swing.

Here's how to do one-handed drills. (Note: You can do these without a ball to practice form, but they're much more effective and fun with a tee!)

You'll need a bat that is lighter and 2 inches shorter than your usual bat (to simulate what you're used to without too much weight) and a tee (optional but recommended).

1. Place your ball on the tee in the same location you would use for a standard middle pitch (bottom of the home plate and center, so the tee is halfway on it).
2. Take a batting stance, but use only your right arm, holding the bat in the spot that you would usually have it in a regular two-handed grip. Your left hand should be behind your back.
3. Hit the ball on the tee, slowly at first, taking care to use the same form that you would in a normal swing. Take note of how your hips give a lot of the swing power and how, without your left arm, you've got great aim but very little power. That will change, but for now, just notice this to better understand the full batting stance and how your hips and arms work together for a swing.
4. Repeat this a few times, then put your right hand behind your back and use your left hand. The ball will be harder to hit, but when you hit it, the *thunk* will be solid.

Do this three times with each arm, and then try a swing with both arms. By practicing this drill, as long as you're careful to stick to proper form, you can make your swing fast, accurate, and powerful. Just be sure to get another player or your coach to help to make sure that your form is correct.

STRATEGIES FOR FACING DIFFERENT TYPES OF PITCHES

When you step up to the plate to bat, you never know what might be coming. While the pitcher may throw a standard, high-velocity pitch that you could conceivably knock out of the park, it's more likely that they're going to try something sneaky.

In the sections below, we'll talk about some types of pitches that you'll encounter — and what you need to do to hit them. After that, we'll talk about how you can get some practice doing this. After all, you're going to need it for those crafty pitches!

Breaking Balls

Breaking balls come at various speeds, but the intent is always the same — they move a little right before they get to the batter. Here are some examples and strategies for hitting them:

> **Curveballs:** One of the most famous breaking balls, curveballs do most of their actual curving in the last 15 feet before they reach the plate. You can also identify them by the red dot that they'll make with their fast-spinning seams. As soon as you see that, change your stance so your feet are shoulder-width apart, with your weight about 70% to the back, before you hit the ball.

> **Sliders:** A slider approaches like a fastball but makes a sharp break as it gets close to home plate. You'll notice a red dot near the 2 o'clock position when it's close, which will be a darker shade of red than most other breaking balls. As it approaches home, it will veer in the direction of the pitcher's dominant hand — right for righties, left for lefties. To hit it, you need to keep your legs firm and extend your arms carefully — don't lunge!

> **Screwballs:** Screwballs can be devastating, but luckily, they're pretty rare — a pitcher can injure their arm if a screwball is not thrown perfectly. This type of pitch can be recognized by its downward trajectory and a very slight rotation of the ball in flight. The trick to hitting a screwball is practice, practice, practice. While they look strange in flight, they're actually not that hard to hit if you keep your cool.

Fastballs

Fastballs are the most common type of pitch that will be lobbed at you. These swift-soaring balls don't give you a lot of time to think, and if you aren't careful, you'll get a strike for your troubles.

Fastballs can be divided into the following three most common types:

2-seam: A 2-seam fastball sinks slightly when thrown, and always moves a little in the direction of the arm that threw it (for instance, a right-handed 2-seamer veers slightly right). That sinking is your hint—you need to hit and follow through a bit lower than you would with a standard pitch, otherwise, you'll hit the ball towards the top. It's called a 2-seam because you'll see two seams when the pitch is released.

4-seam: Fast and with almost no deviation from its path, the trick to these is that there isn't really a trick. You learn to hit them by practicing—the key is recognition and responding quickly without panicking. They're called 4-seams because you'll see all four seams on the ball when it's released.

Cutters: A cutter is thrown so that it heads toward the catcher's mitt as it gets close to home. These can be hard to hit for a right-handed hitter, but you can train by practicing with your tee aligned with the middle of home plate, putting your front foot down, and driving the ball toward the middle of the diamond.

Changeups

Changeups occur when the pitcher throws what appears to be a fastball but is actually nowhere near as fast. These take practice to recognize, as they're designed to throw off the batter's timing.

Examples of changeups include palm balls, fish changes, and Vulcan changeups, and the only way to defeat these is experience. You'll eventually get a feel for the speed of pitches and learn to recognize changeups, but it will take a little time and a lot of practice.

PITCH RECOGNITION EXERCISES

If you're lucky, you might already have a pitcher who can throw some of the more exotic pitches, perhaps your coach or a teammate. If you don't, that's okay—you can still get plenty of practice, you just need to know where to go.

Search the internet to see what's available in your area, and if you like, you can check for a baseball academy in your city, as well. Many businesses have batting cages with pitching machines you can rent, usually used with tokens that you can purchase. These pitching machines give you practice with different types of pitches in real-time, and you can watch the flights over and over until you know them by heart.

After that, opposing pitchers will be in for a big surprise when they meet you on the field!

CHAPTER FIVE: FIELDING SKILLS

In this section, we'll go over some fielding basics to give you a foundation to build on. There's quite a lot to learn about fielding. After you've done some drills and played a few games, you'll see what we mean when we say that, sometimes, baseball has a mind of its own!

With that said, proper technique, an understanding of infield versus outfield fielding skills, communication strategies, and (of course) practice will help you take what you learn here and develop formidable fielding skills.

We'll start things off with your pre-pitch stance, followed by form for fielding grounders and fly balls. After that, we'll move on to proper throwing and catching forms, then clarify the difference between infield and outfield play so you'll know which technique you need to use.

Next, we'll provide some drills to turn that knowledge into muscle memory and, finally, finish up with a crash course in communication that your team can customize to talk during games without giving away your strategy.

BASICS OF FIELDING GROUND AND FLY BALLS

The two most common fielding scenarios come in the form of ground balls and fly balls, so this is the perfect place to start. For each, we'll give you a basic technique to help you capture the ball so you can get it back into play quickly.

Proper Fielding Stance and Glove Position

Your first stance is one of the easiest ones since there's not a lot to it. When you go to your fielding position, here is your pre-pitch stance:

1. To get ready for action, put your feet shoulder-width apart, knees slightly bent, and lean forward a little at your hips. The foot by your glove should be back a little, behind your pitching-arm foot, and your eyes need to be turned toward the catcher.
2. Palms should be relaxed, facing the batter.
3. Some fielders stay planted like a potted fern, but that's not a good habit to get into. As soon as the pitch passes into the hitting zone, two quick steps and a small hop into position help get your blood circulating and prepare you for action. You can do this or substitute an equivalent move of your own—your goal is to move and stay focused.

Fielding Ground Balls

The hardest thing about fielding a ground ball is getting over any worries that it'll pop up and smack you in the noggin. You're going to have to get over it—get your head down and your eyes on the ball and keep them there. Moving your head will make you move your arms, too, and when that happens, you won't be placed right to intercept that ball.

Proper Fielding Stance and Glove Position

1. Center your body toward the incoming ball and put your feet shoulder-width apart, with your throwing-side foot slightly behind the other.
2. Your knees should be bent, with your buttocks at knee level and your back almost parallel to the ground. Stretch your arms out in front of you and point your toes forward.
3. The back of your fielder's glove needs to be on the ground, with your throwing hand close above or beside it, in a way that won't block the ball if it bounces on the glove. This will allow you to trap the incoming ball so you can bring it close and throw it where it needs to go.

Cut and Circle

If the ball is coming toward you from either side, you need to cut an angle toward it—but always move back a little, not forward. If you move forward aggressively, the ball might roll straight past you. Instead, move in a circular pattern and get the back of your glove to the ground to intercept the ball.

If you panic and stab your glove down with the back of the glove toward the ball, it will likely bounce off your glove, and then you'll have to chase it. Above all, keep your cool—if you're not afraid of the ball, you'll be able to scoop it up and take control.

Catching Fly Balls

Catching fly balls is a matter of keeping your eye on the ball and estimating where it's going to land. A player should call the ball as well to help avoid running into a teammate who's also trying to catch the ball:

1. The player nearest to where the ball will land calls the ball.
2. Keeping their eyes on the ball (but noting surroundings), the player reaches the spot where they will catch it, and then the glove goes up. Avoid running with your glove held out, as it will only slow you down. Focus on getting to the drop spot, then plant your feet firmly and stretch out that glove to catch the ball.

TECHNIQUES FOR CATCHING AND THROWING

Below, you'll find tips and techniques to improve your catching and throwing, and while some of them look easy, you'll see the reality of it when you give them a try. The problem with catching boils down to this: Your mind sees a fast-flying object heading your way, and instinct tells you to move or hide behind your glove.

With throwing, it's more about precision, form, and split-second decisions.

By learning these basics and overcoming your fight or flight instincts, you'll develop ways to deal with and relocate a fast-moving ball, along with a good grounding in form and fielding fundamentals that will help you build up to more advanced techniques.

Just remember that you'll need to practice for your responses to become automatic, and that takes time. With that said, here are those tips and techniques.

Catching

Don't Lock Your Elbows: If you lock your elbows in a catch, the ball is likely to bounce right out of your glove. Relax your elbows into a soft catch, which helps absorb force so you can quickly catch and transfer the ball.

Use the Triangle Technique: When you are fielding a grounder and aren't sure about your form, think about a triangle. Your feet should be shoulder-width apart, your knees and hips bent, and the back of your glove front and center—a perfect triangle.

Always Low to High: With ground balls, always start with your glove low. That way, if the ball bounces, you can bring your glove up to catch it with ease. If you start with your glove high, you might panic and stab down at the ball—forcing you to chase it—or the ball might simply roll between your legs.

Don't Turn When You Run: Side-stepping is always better for intercepting because you always need to keep an eye on the ball. While instinct says you'll get there faster if you turn and run as fast as you can, the moment you take your eyes off the ball, anything could happen.

Use Both Hands: Always keep your throwing hand close to your glove, but not in the way. While you can certainly catch a ball just by focusing on your glove hand, you still want to be able to transfer it quickly if needed, so get in the habit of keeping your other hand close.

Throwing

Practice Transfers: When the ball lands in your glove, your other hand should immediately close over it so you can be ready to throw it where it needs to go. This won't take long to become automatic—when the ball lands, capture it, then put it right back in motion.

Find Your Favorite Grip: Usually, you'll be employing a 2-seam or 4-seam grip for a little more power—we'll go over these in the next chapter.

Practice Simple Infield Base Drills: An easy drill to sharpen your quick-thinking and accuracy skills requires your infielders to get into position. Have someone throw the ball at random, and when it's caught, that same person calls a base to throw it to. When the infielder by that base catches the ball, you can call another base and continue, or start over for a nice, basic drill that helps hone your team's skills.

Learn Outfielder Circular Throws: Outfielders have to throw the ball further than infielders, and one technique for this is called a circular throw. When an outfielder catches the ball and transfers it to their pitching hand, that hand should go down by the waist, then back behind, and around and over the top. This circular movement gives the ball more energy, which results in more distance.

INFIELD VS. OUTFIELD FIELDING SKILLS

While it might sound like it, playing an outfield position isn't just playing infield further out. The required skills are actually very different. This is something you need to understand and practice when playing multiple positions.

For infield players, everything is fast and furious. They need to move the ball quickly, so fast pitches designed for shorter distances are the most important to learn. They also cover a tighter area, so they won't be running as much as outfielders.

That doesn't mean infielders aren't busy—they handle the ball more and, in addition to developing fast reflexes, must gauge the tendencies of opposing batters and adjust their running speed to ensure proper defense.

Outfielders, by comparison, need to be good at tracking fast-moving balls, and after catching them, they need a strong throwing arm and good pitching form to ensure the ball cannot only bridge the distance to the infielders but also reach the correct target.

Now that you know both roles better, you can use this information to help you train and identify the areas in which you and your teammates are strong—and where you can improve.

After that, it's practice, practice, practice, and before you know it, your team will be a whole lot more versatile—and much harder to beat!

DRILLS FOR IMPROVING FIELD ACCURACY

To help you practice your fielding accuracy, we've got a pair of starter drills you can use to learn the basics and tweak as your skills grow. We'll provide a drill for fly balls and grounders for now, and later when we get into playing different positions, we'll give you some more targeted drills.

If you're ready, let's get started.

Fly Ball Cones

While you could just practice catching fly balls by going out and having someone throw them to you, using a more organized drill like fly ball cones will get you a lot more training mileage. You can adjust the difficulty level by adding more cones and distance, and having those physical markers helps you gauge your strengths and weaknesses a lot more easily.

For this exercise, you'll need at least three orange traffic cones (or other easy-to-see markers). Once you have those, follow these steps:

1. Arrange the cones in a straight line, with 20 feet between each cone.
2. At each cone, the coach throws ten balls, each cone having a difficulty level. The first cone will be the easiest (underarm or low overarm throws), with a little more height and velocity for the second cone, and the third being the hardest. The coach should start 15-20 feet away, eventually moving up to 30 feet away for future drills.

This simple drill will get you used to fielding balls from different angles, and once you've mastered three cones, you can add more cones to upgrade the drill. Additionally, you can create fun variations, such as having more players who can also practice calling "Ball!" when they're in the best position to catch the fly ball.

Grounder Track and Call

The grounder track and call is a nice, basic ground ball drill designed to help you get in the habit of keeping your eyes on the ball and practice working as a team. When the ball goes into play, the closest player should call it before catching it.

It's not a matter of who calls first—everyone needs to learn to function as a team, and that means getting into the habit of tracking the ball and trusting each other to cover their own areas. We'll give you the basics, and you can make modifications to increase difficulty as you go:

1. Have 3-5 players lay belly down at a distance, gloves in front, and watch for grounders that will be tossed their way.
2. When the pitcher throws the ball, they call, "Up!" as a cue for everyone to jump up. The player closest to the ball then calls, "Ball!" and assumes the triangle capture position—feet shoulder-width apart, back of the glove front and center on the ground—to catch the ball and throw it back.
3. If two players call the ball, it's up to the rest of the team to shout the name of the player they think is closest to the ball. Then, that player intercepts the ground ball and throws it back.

This may seem simplistic, but it's great practice. The whole team needs to be aware of the ball—and who is closest to it. Developing trust early on allows for more complex versions of the exercise, where players will be in their regular positions, and each one will intuitively know which areas are covered defensively.

In later versions of the drill, players can start in a standing position, and you can add difficulties—like keeping their eyes closed until the pitch is called. You get the idea. Like a lot of exercises in this book, this is a drill you can customize as you and your teammates get better and better.

Speaking of calling the ball, it's time to touch on communication skills—another crucial part of functioning as a team.

COMMUNICATING WITH TEAMMATES ON THE FIELD

These days, Major League Baseball (MLB) players have the technology to communicate remotely during games. However, baseball has a long history of non-tech communication that's still used often.

In our grounder drill, we practiced calling the ball and having players call out the name of the player they thought was closest to the ball. That's good for drilling, but there's a lot more to baseball communication than that.

For instance, if two players are close to catching a ball—let's say it was a shallow hit into left field, and both the shortstop and the left fielder have called it—the left fielder could say, "Get out!" and catch the ball themselves. The left field is their area, after all.

Another common phrase you'll hear is the very practical call of "Watch out!" when a teammate is about to run into something they didn't see because they're watching the ball.

Infielders often use verbal communication—for instance, shouting, "Cut one!" means to cut a throw and, instead, to pitch the ball to first base, with "Cut two" referring to second, and so on.

Your coach will usually have preferred terms to use, but these work to give you the basic idea. Using specific phrases to communicate with your team helps you work together better to win games. Additionally, players will often designate a hot sign for the team to use, which is a word or a specific signal (such as tapping your helmet a certain way) to get the attention of the other players.

Other teams may figure out your internal team language during the game, but you can prevent this by having a backup hot sign that means you're switching to a different code.

It's up to you and your team how much time you spend developing this, but this type of coded communication can be very effective for executing practiced plays and switching strategies during games.

Non-verbal signals are also important. Certain hand signals can indicate specific plays, for instance, or you might have something that mimics regular body language. For instance, if you give a teammate a coded command, they might shrug their shoulders in a way that looks like they didn't get the message—but that's for the other team, as you'll know that this shrug means they understood.

Experiment and get in the habit of using your hot sign to make sure your teammates are paying attention and practice the signal for "understood."

Developing a team language takes time, but this is a great way to be sneaky during games, and once you get the hang of it, you'll be amazed at the difference it can make.

CHAPTER SIX: THROWING AND PITCHING

Being able to throw a proper pitch is a must, and once you've got it down, various grips can allow you to throw more challenging and sneakier pitches against batters and for formidable fielding.

We'll start by teaching you, step by step, how to pitch, and from there, we'll go into different grips and techniques, safety tips, and drills. Then, we'll top things off with a quick intro to advanced pitching styles.

PROPER THROWING MECHANICS

A proper pitch is all about form. It requires wind up, hip motion, and arm extension in a circular motion. Your entire body needs to be pointed and focused on high-speed delivery. For the purposes of this explanation, the "glove side" and "lead" leg/foot refer to your non-dominant side, the opposite of your pitching arm—left if you're right-handed, right if you're left-handed—while the "pivot foot" is on the dominant side.

To help you understand proper throwing mechanics, we've broken the pitching process up into nine steps:

1. Looking straight ahead, your feet should be shoulder-width apart and your elbows at your sides, with the ball held to the center of your chest, hidden behind your glove.
2. Step slightly to your glove (non-dominant) side. Press the side of your pivot foot against the pitching rubber behind you.
3. Lift your lead (non-dominant) knee waist-high, letting your other leg bend slightly at the knee for more power in your pitch. In the correct position, the buttocks of your lead leg should face the home plate. Keep your hands up, close to your shoulder.

4. Bring the ball down by your hip as you bring your glove around and wind your torso back. Your body should now be facing toward third base (if you are right-handed) or first base (if you are left-handed).
5. Bring your glove-side foot down, almost to the ground (but not quite), then stretch it out to stride toward home plate, bringing your pitching arm back behind you, parallel to the ground.
6. Angle your lead foot down 75 degrees as it comes down for your stride — this is important.
7. Push from your pivot foot while lifting your lead foot into a 90-degree upward angle to help pull you forward.
8. Twisting your torso, stretch your glove arm forward across your body, lifting your elbow up by your shoulder for the throw. Bring your pitching arm forward and let the ball roll out of your hands into the pitch. Don't pull your wrist back — this is a good way to injure your pitching arm. Instead, let the motion from your pivot and twist guide the ball to roll at high velocity from your pitching hand.
9. Bring your back (dominant) leg up as you pitch to give your arm full extension — that 90-degree angle in your lead foot will brace you to get into a ready fielding position at the termination of the pitch.

Pitching is tricky to learn, so get your friends and your coach to help. You can also look at the stance from many angles on the internet to help you practice. While you might already be able to pitch passably well, learning proper form will make you even better, so don't skip this step.

BASIC PITCHING TECHNIQUES

As a pitcher, your grip is important — it allows you to control the speed of the ball so you can throw some amazing pitches. We'll give you four different grips to start practicing so you can get an idea of how devastating these pitches can be.

2-Seam Fastball Grip

A 2-seam fastball grip gives you a good bit of power, and it's easy to do. Place your index and middle fingers along the seams on the narrowest side of the baseball stitching. Your thumb should be under the ball, and when you throw this right, the ball should sink slightly on release.

This will take a little practice, but it's all about the angle on release, so try this one out with a friend so you can both learn to throw this pitch and how to recognize it when you're at bat.

4-Seam Fastball Grip

The 4-seam fastball grip is a favorite of many pitchers—it flies in fast and straight, with a vicious backspin. To perform a four-seam grip, your index and middle fingers should be ½ to 1 inch apart at the top of the ball, perpendicular to one of the U-shaped seams. For easy visualization, look for the seams to make the shape of a smile under your fingers, with the shape of a frown by your thumbs.

The trick to this pitch is to give the ball a backspin on release, so let it roll to your fingertips at release to get that spin going.

Curveball Grip

Everyone has heard of the dreaded curveball, so you'll definitely want to learn to throw one. To achieve this grip, place your middle and index fingers close together, pressed tightly against the seam, and position your thumb on the opposite seam, lined up with your middle finger.

Rather than at the top and middle (like the previous pitches), with the curveball grip, your top fingers should be on the side of the ball. This allows you to pull down hard as you release the ball to give it that extra topspin needed for its trademark curve.

Changeup Grip

A changeup pitch goes slower than the batter will be expecting, since the pitch itself resembles that of a fastball, with a little added movement. To perform a changeup grip, space your middle, ring, and pinky fingers across the top of the ball, supporting it with your thumb, and press your index finger to your thumb. Basically, you'll be making the 'okay' sign, but with your thumb supporting the bottom of the ball.

To use this pitch, just throw it like you would a fastball. The different grip will make the ball come in slower, but the style of your throw could trick the batter into swinging early since they'll be expecting a fastball — that's why it's called a "changeup."

These four pitches will get you started, but don't worry — we're not done yet. At the end of this chapter, we'll introduce a few more advanced pitches.

Importance of Arm Care and Injury Prevention

Pitching is hard on your arms and shoulders, so always make sure to warm up and stretch before pitching and perform cool-down exercises afterward. Here are some additional tips to help avoid arm injury as a pitcher:

Observe Pitching Limits: Ages 7-8 should pitch no more than 50 times in one day, ages 9-10 no more than 75 times per day, and ages 11-12 may pitch up to 85 times per day.

Every year, pitchers need to take four months off from pitching, and at least two — preferably three — of those months need to be consecutive (in a row).

When pitchers aren't pitching, they shouldn't be catchers. Both positions place a lot of strain on the arms, so catching during these pitching breaks increases the likelihood of injury.

Avoid pitching more than one game in the same day, and if you have multiple games in the same week, each pitcher should pitch for no more than two days in a row.

Never pitch when you're tired or if your arm is hurting. Give yourself time to recover, and have your coach put someone else in play while you rest.

IMPROVING THROWING ACCURACY AND STRENGTH

Now that you have some grips to play with, we need to work on accuracy and strength. As with most skills, these can only be gained through a combination of good form and, of course, practice.

Below, you'll find three practical drills to improve your pitching, along with some info about each one. That way, you'll know what we're focusing on and how these drills can help.

Windup Balance Drill

Getting your pitching stance right can be a pain at first. Even if you watch a video, it's not always easy to imitate with your body what you see with your eyes. When you're just starting to learn proper form, it's easy to get excited and rush the steps.

The problem is that rushing can lead to a bad-form pitch and, even worse, injury. The good news is that the windup balance drill is a good way to help you gain confidence and practice with proper form so you can pitch accurately under stress.

To practice a windup balance drill, follow these steps:

1. Line up and start a pitching stance—this can be with or without a ball, but it's easier with one.

2. At the portion of the windup when your knee is raised, freeze in place.
3. Hold this pose for a couple of seconds and check to make sure your knee is at least waist high.
4. Repeat this exercise 15 times during practice, and again before each game.
1. Not only will this drill improve your balance, but it also helps ensure you're using the proper form and improves the quality of your pitches.

Sitting Pitches Drill

Accuracy is important for pitchers, and one way to develop this while also strengthening the body is the sitting pitches drill. You'll need a friend to catch for this one, so make sure they're properly outfitted, with a helmet and catcher's padding.

Here's what you need to do:

1. Sit on the ground with your legs crossed and have your catcher friend do the same 20 to 30 feet away.
2. Have the catcher hold their glove in front of them while you throw 20 pitches at their glove from this sitting position.
3. Your goal is to get the ball to its target without bouncing off the ground, with as little rocking motion as possible.

This is great exercise for your shoulder, and it's also valuable for polishing up your pitching technique. Provided you've both got safety gear that fits properly, you and your friend can switch roles to practice both positions.

Short Pitch Practice Drill

It's easier to make mistakes over a distance, and what's worse, it's harder to figure out what went wrong. A good solution for this is a little short-pitch practice. You'll need to pair up with your catcher friend again to practice this drill, then follow these steps:

1. Stand about 45 feet away from your catcher friend.
2. When the catcher is ready, try each pitch you know for ten throws. Take a brief rest between sets of ten. Remember, there's no rush—the important thing is to pay attention to form.
3. After going through all your pitches, put on your catcher's gear and switch with your friend so they can practice their pitches.

This drill seems simple, but throwing your pitches at a shorter distance not only helps to build confidence, but it can also help you catch errors more easily. With longer distances, there's more time between throws, and it's harder to figure out where you went wrong.

Make sure to do a full windup and throw normally during this drill. The repetition helps you focus on form and catch errors as you build up strength and experience. With a bit of practice, your form will improve, and you'll see the difference in your full-distance throws.

INTRO TO ADVANCED PITCHING TECHNIQUES

Before we close out this chapter, we have three more pitches to show you as an introduction to advanced pitching techniques. Just keep in mind that, while we can tell you how to grip and how to throw each pitch, these take a lot of practice to get the hang of, and a little independent study is required on your part to fully master them.

We recommend looking up videos on the internet once you've got the grip down, and you should ask your coach for help practicing these pitches. Finally, you can have a friend record a video during practice so you can watch your pitches and check for things like form and release.

One great thing about having videos of yourself is that you can slow down the playback speed, which makes it easier to spot your mistakes. With that said, let's take a look at those advanced pitches.

Knuckleball Grip

Knuckleballs are tricky to throw, but they're even harder to hit—they end up all over the place in the strike zone. This grip requires you to put your middle and index fingers on top of the ball, with your knuckles up and your fingertips gripping the baseball. Your pinky finger should dangle off to the side, while your thumb supports the ball underneath.

When you throw a knuckleball, the key is to keep your wrist stiff at release until the ball has completely left your hand. This will send your knuckleball out with little to no spin, and if you do it right, the batter is about to have a very bad day!

Knuckle Curveball Grip

A knuckle curveball is another super-sneaky pitch designed to go from high to low on the strike zone, with a slight curve and a slower velocity than a regular curveball. The grip can feel a little weird, though, until you get used to it.

For a knuckle curveball grip, you'll need to curl your index finger, so your fingernail presses against the top of the ball, support the bottom with your thumb, and space your remaining three fingers to center the ball.

Use your folded index finger to point at your target and be sure to hide your grip with your glove before you pitch. Throw using a standard pitch with a snap at the release, and your knuckle curveball is officially launched!

Slider

A slider is a useful part of your pitcher's arsenal because it looks like a fastball but will veer toward your glove side and drop a bit at the plate. This can result in the batter making a weak contact or even missing the ball completely.

To throw a slider, put your index and middle finger together and look for the horseshoe on your seams. Place your middle finger on the bottom of the U-shape, leaving your index finger touching only the leather. Curl your ring and pinky fingers at the side, and support the ball with your thumb, then release it as though you're throwing a football.

This grip allows you to pull down on release, spinning the ball to the side like a top. When you get it right, the ball will fly out towards your glove-hand side, dropping a little at the plate. Be patient with this one—it takes a long time to learn to throw a decent slider, but it's definitely worth it.

CHAPTER SEVEN: BASERUNNING SKILLS

Most of you know the most basic aspects: There are four bases, arranged in a diamond pattern, and when you hit a ball, you must run to each base in the correct counterclockwise order, touching each base with your foot (or, in a pinch, your hand!).

However, there are other things to keep in mind as well, such as the fact that it's okay if you run to a base and only manage to stop a few feet past it — provided you don't continue on to the next base. Two runners cannot occupy the same space, either, so if you both get tagged, the lead runner is out.

We should also mention that, when stealing bases, be sure to tag up, which means that, in the case of a fly ball, you must stay on (or return to) the base you're occupying until the ball touches the fielder's glove.

These are all pretty basic aspects of running bases, so this chapter will expand on topics like leading off and stealing bases, tips for sliding safely, reading pitchers and fielders, and practice drills, then we'll finish up with advice on baserunning strategy.

Ready to up your game? Then let's get started!

LEADING OFF AND STEALING BASES

Base stealing is fun, and there's an art to it that players must perfect over time. Like anything, you want to start things off on the right foot. As far as stealing bases is concerned, that's knowing how to lead off.

Leading off is simply taking a few steps from the base right before the pitcher throws. This gives you an edge in making a run for the next base, but also keeps you close enough that you can retreat to safety if the pitcher figures out what you're up to.

The proper stance for a lead off looks like this:

1. Take a big step out with your dominant foot.
2. Your other foot should be behind you, so you have a wide stance.
3. Crouch down with your hands in front of you.
4. Feel free to shuffle a bit to put a little panic in the infielder's mind!

We aren't kidding about that panic bit. When you lead off, everyone knows you might try to steal a base—but you also might not. No one knows except you, of course, and that added tension is great for making the other team nervous.

Once you're in place, you need to focus on the pitcher. In fact, when you're in the dugout, you should be studying them as well. Get a good idea of their body language when they're about to pick off another player trying to steal a base and learn what you can before it's your turn at the bat.

After that, it's mostly going to be about timing. Another thing to keep in mind is that, if you run to steal a base, a lot of infielders will start keeping an eye on you—and if your teammate gets a solid hit in, those distracted fielders will have more than one thing to worry about!

Stealing Bases

Of course, there's a whole lot more to stealing bases, but most of it will be learned firsthand. With that said, here are a few tried and true tips to sharpen up your steals:

> **Get a Stopwatch, and Use It:** When you're in the dugout, use your stopwatch to time how long a pitcher's throw takes to get to home, along with how long it takes a catcher to throw to second base. You want to know how much time you'll have to work with, and this is how you figure it out.
>
> **Is the Pitcher a Lefty or Righty?** A right-handed pitcher can pick you off a lot easier at third base than at second, and the

reverse is true for left-handed pitchers. Keep this in mind, and adjust your strategy as needed.

Use Those Shuffle Steps: Shuffling steps move you a little closer to the base you plan to steal, and they're also great to psych out the other team. Don't waste that momentum—when you're ready to steal, use it to help you get to top running speed more quickly.

Stealing Third Base is Usually Easier Than Stealing Second: You'll use a bigger lead at third base than you would at second, and statistically, it's an easier steal. Just be sure you've studied the catcher and pitcher, so you know what to expect.

Be Realistic About How Fast You Really Are: That stopwatch you used before comes in handy for timing yourself, too. No matter how fast you or your teammates think you are, if you don't know, then you aren't calculating—you're guessing.

Eight Tips for Sliding Safely

Safety is paramount when it comes to sliding. Not only do you need to observe proper form and get in a lot of practice to slide safely, but also to slide effectively. You want your slide to be as carefully controlled as possible. No matter how cool your slide looks, if you don't observe a few basic rules, you'll come in too slowly—or predictably.

We've compiled some sliding tips to help you stay safe from harm and, with a little luck, that infielder who's trying to get you:

Sliding Shorts are Your Friend: Sliding shorts provide an extra layer of padding between your hips and the ground. While they're not usually required, that added protection is useful and helps new players overcome their fear of trying a slide.

Extend Your Leg First: When you go into a slide, extend the leg closest to the base so your foot leads as you slide into the base.

Back Knee at 90 Degrees: Your other leg provides support while sliding, and you should bend that knee at a 90-degree angle. If you don't, you might end up jerking to a stop as it gets caught on the base.

Always Aim for the Corner: Don't target the exact center of the base when you slide in. Since it's common sense to aim for the closest target, go for the corner—as long as your foot touches the base before you get tagged, you're golden!

Compact Your Body on Approach: Since you'll be sliding on the ground, lower your body upon approach to prepare. This helps you avoid injury, as your body has less distance to fall, and it gives you better control of the slide.

Use Your Hands (but Don't Reach!): It's okay to use your arms for balance, but never reach out further than you need to. Overextending your arms on a slide can result in injured hands or fingers, so keep your arms close. Holding your palms out in front of you protects your arms while giving you enough control at the same time.

Only Slide when Necessary: Sliding is fun, but if you do it every time, you'll become predictable. Reserve slides as an ace up your sleeve, like when you need to avoid a tag or want to steal a base.

Wet Grass and Sliding Drills Can Teach You a Lot: You can practice sliding in your own backyard, provided the grass is thick enough. Use a hose to wet it a little in advance, and it can be a fun and effective training tool.

READING PITCHERS AND FIELDERS

Baseball legend Ty Cobb is well-known as an amazing hitter, but did you know that he's also considered one of the greatest baserunners of all time? In fact, he's stolen so many bases that players on opposing teams would often worry when he was dusting himself off at a base, even though he wasn't poised to make a run for it.

The reason Ty was so good was simple: He'd made a habit of watching the pitchers and fielders. What's more, he studied batters' crack to estimate how far the ball might go, while keeping those defensive fielders in his sights.

Below, you'll find some tips to help you create your own plan for reading pitchers and fielders in order to anticipate the best times for stealing bases:

Reading Pitchers

Learn About Pitching Grips: 2-seam grips work for sinkers, while 4-seam grips are good for fastballs. Details like this can help you anticipate what pitch to expect. You'll be familiar with the batter's strengths and weaknesses already, so if you notice specific grips, you'll have a good idea about what might happen next.

Release Points and Spin: Knowing when a ball is released is important for guessing what throw it is and how it'll spin. This takes practice, but a sharp eye can help you spot the more devious pitches so you can decide whether it's a good time to steal a base or not.

Watch the Windup: The pitcher's form and windup can tell you a lot about the power of the throw that will follow.

Always Study the Pitchers: All pitchers have favorite throws for certain situations, such as throwing a breaking ball on a 0-2 count consistently. If the pitcher broadcasts any obvious patterns, you should be aware of them.

Reading Fielders

Staying Still or Active: Many fielders hop when a pitch is about to be hit to prepare for action. However, you'll spot inactive fielders occasionally. If a ball goes to them, they're likely to respond sluggishly, which can work in your favor — if you're watching for it.

Know Your Foe: Every player has their strengths and weaknesses, and it's up to you to learn them. Some fielders run slower than others, have a less powerful pitch, tend to guard poorly or fail to stay in their assigned position. It's up to you to punish them for it by using these weaknesses to your advantage.

Scouting Reports

Scouting reports are amazing tools used to assess baserunning, hitting, fielding, and pitching, but they also assess how individual players and their teams work together.

In pro baseball, scouts use these reports to recruit new players, but they're also used in youth baseball. In fact, if your coach is more experienced, you might already know that scouting reports can provide incredibly useful information for improving your game and scoping out opposing teams.

Several third-party organizations create scouting reports by watching games and practices to help get everyone to see the bigger picture, and they're worth it.

Check with your coach to find out if this is something they're doing or might consider doing. Not only can it improve your personal game, but if your coach has been collecting intel on other teams, you'll be able to prepare more viable strategies for baserunning and much, much more.

Don't Forget the Batters

On a final note, don't forget Ty Cobb's other winning habit of listening for the crack of the bat on an incoming ball. Home run hits have a fuller sound, and glancing hits to the ball are easy to recognize, as well—all without even looking.

You'll also know your own batters, so combine that knowledge with some active listening for the sound of the hit, and you'll quickly develop an edge that can take you far.

IMPROVING BASERUNNING SPEED AND AGILITY

Now that you've got some tips to work with, it's time to practice your baserunning skills with some drills. We've included two drills in this section. The first is designed to tighten up your form and get you used to running the bases, while the second exercise will help with leading off and tagging up.

Before we proceed, we should mention that the Figure 8 drill in Chapter 3 is also excellent for improving your baserunning agility. With that said, let's take a look at those two new drills.

Basic Baserunning Drill

As with all athletic skills, learning proper form is fundamental to developing good baserunning habits. While performing this drill, keep these things in mind:

> **Target the corner of the base—not the center—**and turn by placing the left arm across the chest, turning your shoulders with it (to the right), while the hips and legs turn left (the opposite way). This helps you round the base, coiling up power as you make the turn.

Remember, a diamond is basically a square turned on its corner. For some people, thinking about it this way makes it easier to visualize those sharp angles you need to master.

When you reach a base, practice tagging it on the inside corner with your left foot. Don't force it, but keep it in mind — eventually, it'll become instinctual, making the whole process feel more natural.

How to perform the baserunning basics drill:

1. Divide your team into four groups and have one group line up halfway between each base. One group should be between home and first, the next between first and second, and so on.
2. Start the drill by having the first person in each line walk the bases from their starting point, going to the end of the next line before continuing.
3. Once each player has walked all the bases a few times, repeat the drill at a jog, then increase to ¾ speed, and finally, a full run.

This drill establishes the movement physics of baserunning until it becomes a matter of muscle memory. Focus on form while making those turns, and once it becomes automatic, you'll be prepared to run bases while staying aware of the players around you.

Lead-Off and Tag-Up

Getting in the habit of leading off and tagging up allows you to steal bases without accidentally earning yourself an out. This simple drill can help you develop this habit, so here's how it's done:

1. Place players on first, second, and third bases, with both a pitcher and catcher in position.
2. When the pitcher throws, each player leads off and tags up, so they've touched their bases and are now a little ahead, ready for a run.

3. As soon as the catcher gets the ball and shouts, "Go!" each player runs to the next base at full speed.
4. When they arrive, each player touches the next base with their foot, and then, the process repeats.

This drill helps players get in the habit of touching the base, leading off, and tagging up so you won't have to worry about an out that, with practice, could have easily been avoided.

Some Final Strategies for Effective Baserunning

It's time for us to move on, but before we close out this chapter on baserunning, we've got a few more tips and strategies to keep in mind.

First off, we want to emphasize the importance of hitting the corner of the base with your left foot. While it takes getting used to, this keeps you from losing momentum when you need to turn quickly—it puts you in position to cross your right foot over to shift course toward the next base.

When it comes to stealing bases, always remember to be aware of the ball's position. Little details—like how it takes longer to throw a ball from right field to third base than it does from left field—can help you develop good base-stealing instincts.

Also, when you're on first base, avoid the temptation of trying to steal second off a fly ball. In most cases, the ball won't be deep enough in the outfield, and if so, it's a very short throw to second base.

Finally, drill as much as you can to prepare your body for the game, and don't forget to stretch and warm up before and after every practice or game. Over time, your body will toughen up, and once you've got muscle memory on your side, you'll have the focus you need to develop some wicked base-stealing strategies of your own!

CHAPTER EIGHT: PLAYING DIFFERENT POSITIONS

Baseball has nine positions, and you and your teammates need to learn them all if you're going to work together effectively. To help with this, we're starting off this section with an overview of these field positions, sharing the unique responsibilities and skills needed for each.

Even if you won't be playing most of these positions, you need to know how they work and what's expected of each player in these roles. As a flexible player, you'll be an asset to your team, and you'll be able to outsmart opposing players in these roles!

Below is a list of the nine baseball positions. In the sections that follow, we'll tell you what you need to know about each one.

1. Pitcher
2. Catcher
3. First Base
4. Second Base
5. Third Base
6. Shortstop
7. Left Field
8. Center Field
9. Right Field

PITCHER

Positioned right in the middle of the diamond, the pitcher works with the catcher, pitching the ball to strike out the batter or force hits that put their team at a disadvantage. The pitcher is sometimes considered the fifth infielder, as they're the first point of contact for bunts, pop-ups, and infield grounders.

Primary skills needed:

- Throwing strength and accuracy
- Overall body strength
- Overall stamina

- Resistance to pressure
- Strong focus

CATCHER

Positioned directly behind home plate, the catcher communicates with the pitcher to suggest throws, and they catch the ball when it's thrown. Catchers also defend against baserunners and communicate things like plays, outs, and strikes during games.

Primary skills needed:

- Catching ability
- Leadership qualities
- Strong legs
- Overall stamina
- Throwing strength and accuracy

FIRST BASEMAN

Positioned at the first baseline to guard the base, the first baseman gets the most action outside of the catcher and pitcher, with a primary goal of catching the ball first. They don't have to have the most accurate throw, but they need good catching skills and fast reflexes to keep up with all the action.

Primary skills needed:

- Catching ability
- Fielding ground balls properly
- Good reach to catch a ball
- Keeping their foot on the base

SECOND BASEMAN

The second baseman guards second base from between first and second. They need to be good at both catching and throwing, as they're important for double plays and fielding any balls that come in between first and second. It's also easier if they're right-handed—lefties have a harder time with this position due to the way the diamond is arranged.

Primary skills needed:

- Lightning reflexes
- Speed and good footwork
- Fielding ground balls
- Courage

THIRD BASEMAN

The third baseman is positioned along the third baseline, and they have to touch base often to score outs. Aside from this, they're responsible for balls that get hit to the third baseline, and they need quick reflexes to help score outs at first and prevent double plays.

Primary skills needed:

- Glove arm strength
- Lightning reflexes
- Courage
- Good balance

SHORTSTOP

You'll find the shortstop between second and third base, and while they're responsible for balls that come between those bases, they've got a lot more area to cover—they also work extensively with outfielders. Shortstops need a wide assortment of skills, as you'll see below.

Primary skills needed:

- Agility
- Lightning-fast reflexes
- Throwing strength and accuracy
- Catching ability
- Field awareness
- Game awareness

LEFT FIELDER

The left fielder covers an entire third of the outfield from the left side beyond the diamond. As most batters are right-handed, left fielders deal with the most hits, and they need strong throwing arms—they throw to third base often, along with home plate.

Primary skills needed:

- Catching fly balls
- Throwing accuracy
- Speed and good footwork
- Excellent depth perception
- Putting balls that hit the wall back into play

CENTER FIELDER

Outside the diamond and responsible for the center-third of the outfield, the center fielder needs stamina, as they cover the largest portion of the outfield. Players in this position need speed, stamina, and strong arms because they do a lot of running and throwing.

Primary skills needed:

- Leadership qualities
- Arm strength
- Catching fly balls
- Speed and good footwork
- Excellent depth perception
- Putting balls that hit the wall back into play

RIGHT FIELDER

The right fielder is also positioned outside the diamond, responsible for the remaining right third of the outfield. This position requires a lot of running and long throws, as the right fielder does things like preventing triple plays, catching fly balls, and backing up the first baseman. They also throw the occasional fastball to third base when needed.

Primary skills needed:

- Patience
- Field awareness
- Throwing strength
- Catching fly balls
- Excellent depth perception

TRANSITIONING BETWEEN POSITIONS

You'll learn new positions in both practice and live play, so to keep you from getting discouraged, we've compiled a few tips to help while you're learning. Here are some things to keep in mind:

Pacing is good. You can certainly try all the different positions, but it's better to start with one infield and one outfield position that play to your current strengths to build confidence before you start switching things up.

Key defensive positions like first base and catcher are harder than they might look. If you're new to baseball, beef up your skills before playing these positions, or you might get discouraged.

Some positions require more strength and agility than others. For instance, middle positions like second base, shortstop, and center fielder need to move and throw more, while corner spots like first base, third base, left field, and right field are a little more relaxed.

Look at the skill requirements we listed above and be honest with yourself about what you need to work on. That way, you can target positions geared toward your strengths, and if you want to try others, you'll know exactly what skills you need to improve for a chance to earn that spot.

DRILLS FOR EACH POSITION

When you are getting started, your best approach for drilling is going to be "quartering" the positions so they look something like this:

- Catcher drills
- Pitching drills
- Infielder position drills
- Outfielder position drills

This makes it easier to select drills that are more effective for your entire team, and since you have a list of individual requirements for each position, each player can perform specific drills individually to improve the skills needed for their position.

Using our quartering strategy, select which drills your team needs with each category's specific goals in mind. We'll show you in the sections below how that should play out.

Catcher Drills

Catching drills need to be focused on catching the ball and throwing it to each base. That boils down to catching the ball while remaining stationary, along with footwork for throwing to each individual base.

Pitching Drills

Pitching drills should focus on specific pitches, pickoff moves and developing the ability to quickly field bunts and pop-ups that often come the pitcher's way.

Infielder Position Drills

From backhands to moving side to side, infielders need to practice their footwork to deliver precise cutoff throws and keep double plays at bay. Don't forget to practice dealing with grounders, because infielders do a lot of that, too.

Outfielder Position Drills

Outfielders need endurance drills because they'll be chasing a lot of fly balls. That's not all, of course—outfielders also need to practice getting the ball to the infield quickly and accurately to cut off opposing players trying to steal bases.

By taking a blanket approach to these quartered skill focuses, you can develop the overall skills needed for both infield and outfield, while also covering the heavy aspects of catching and fielding. After that, it's just a matter of taking inventory of the skills required for each position and assessing each individual player to learn their strengths and weaknesses.

This will help develop your team in two ways: It allows you to identify exactly which skills the most players in your team need to work on while zeroing in on which skills each individual player needs. That way, the coach can assign specific drills for each player to run on their own or during an allotted time at the end of each practice session.

Our final advice on training for multiple positions is not to forget about warm-up and cool-down time, which are critical for preventing injury.

When you subtract those from your overall anticipated training time per session, the rules we've provided in this section should help you prioritize and build a training regimen tailored to your team's specific needs.

VERSATILITY AND FLEXIBILITY

While there might be positions you hate to play, you need to get in the habit of doing your very best. In baseball, you're part of a team, and your team is counting on you to step up and help.

Even if a certain position isn't your favorite, you should step up and do your best to help your team score points and put up a powerful, unified defense. Don't take our word for it, though — there are concrete benefits from taking this approach.

You'll exercise muscles you might not use often, which will make you stronger and faster over time — but more importantly, playing different positions teaches you invaluable things about how baseball works at a strategic level.

For instance, say you're batting, and you hit a ball to the shortstop. If you've played that position before, you'll know that the ball will likely go straight to second base.

There's a difference between reading about something and actually experiencing it. When you practice playing different positions, you'll eventually perform well in each, and it's easier to defend against a position when you're familiar with it.

FINDING THE BEST POSITION FOR YOU

Now that you know which skills are associated with each different position, you should have a better idea of which positions are good for you. If you still aren't sure, the easiest way to figure it out is to get with your teammates and start rating each other's skills.

Start easy, with a list that looks something like this:

- Catching skill
- Reflexes and Reaction time
- Running speed
- Throwing distance
- Throwing speed

Design a sheet like this, assigning values from 1 to 10 for each skill, and print one out for each teammate so everyone on the team can rate their skills. You can keep one, of course, but having everyone else's opinion of your skills will give you a more honest assessment.

These rankings will tell you where you are in each of these skills, which can help you determine which position you're best suited for. They'll also tell you the most important thing you need to know as a member of a soon-to-be-winning team—where you need to improve to be your very best.

On a final note, an internet search for "free scouting report template" will turn up printable forms for you and your team to rate your skills in more detail—but for now, stick with the basic list. The bullet points above give you a great starting point to build on.

CHAPTER NINE: GAME STRATEGIES AND TACTICS

Understanding the rules of any sport you play is important, and while you probably know the basics of baseball already, there might be a few youth league rules you aren't yet aware of. These guidelines are designed to keep morale high and put safety first, but also to make sure the game stays fun for everyone.

Below is a quick summary, followed by an explanation of each associated rule and why it's important.

- Everybody Plays
- Observe the Pitch Limit
- A Substitution and Re-entry Rule
- Intentionally Walking a Player
- Batter's Box Foot Rule
- The Civilized Call and why it's important
- Everybody Plays

Everyone should get a turn at bat and some time on the field — that's what you're there for, after all! Many Little Leagues have a rule to this effect, making it mandatory that everybody plays.

It's a simple rule. For any team with 12 or fewer players, each player is put into play for six consecutive defense outs — meaning six times in one of the nine defensive positions — and each player gets at least one turn at bat.

If the team has 13 or more members, then everyone is only guaranteed one time at bat. This rule is normally used in tournaments, and it's taken pretty seriously — both team's managers will be warned that, if they don't follow this rule, it could mean getting kicked out of the tournament!

OBSERVE THE PITCH LIMIT

As we mentioned in Chapter 6, a pitching limit for younger players helps prevent injuries. In a nutshell, ages 7–8 should pitch no more than 50 times in one day, ages 9–10 no more than 75 times per day, and ages 11–12 may pitch up to 85 times per day.

There is one exception to this rule, however. If a pitcher has hit their limit but is still facing a batter, they may continue pitching until one of these conditions occurs:

- That batter hits the ball and gets to a base.
- That batter hits the ball, then gets an out.
- A third out completes the half-inning or game.

A Substitution and Re-entry Rule

There are two rules to remember regarding substitutions. First, any substitute entering the game may not be removed until they have completed their mandatory play requirements. Secondly, any player who has been removed by that substitute may re-enter the game in the same batting order as before.

Intentionally Walking a Player

Another rule that's designed to boost player morale is allowing intentional walking. Defensive teams can ask the umpire to walk a batter. This is noted, and instead of receiving a pitch, that batter will take first base. No other players can steal bases during this time, though they may advance if first base is already occupied.

Finally, after the defense walks a batter, they must add four pitches to the defensive pitcher's count to balance this play.

Batter's Box Foot Rule

This rule requires batters to keep both feet within the batter's box. Some batters try to put one foot out to get behind home plate, but this gives them an unfair hitting advantage.

Both feet need to be within the batter's box, or at least touching the line. Umpires watch for this, and a batter will be given one warning. If they step out again, the umpire can call a strike. The warning and the strike must be consecutive, so if you're warned and get another turn at bat later, that warning doesn't count towards an instant strike—but it's best to just keep your feet inside the batter's box.

Finally, if the ball is hit with one or both feet outside the batter's box, the umpire can and will call a strike. Practice staying in the batter's box, and this won't be an issue.

Note: There are some exceptions, so consult your local Little League rules to see which rules apply.

THE CIVILIZED CALL/ 15-RUN RULE

Since Little League players are still learning to play, a rule was developed to reduce the time of the game and keep morale high. The 15-run rule basically states that if the visiting team is 15 runs ahead by the third inning—or the home team is 15 runs ahead halfway through the second inning—the manager of the team with fewer points may call the game.

If this happens while players are still on base and a walk-off home run has been hit, the players on each base count toward the final score.

Basic Offensive and Defensive Strategies

Beating the opposing team isn't just about practicing all the time—it also involves outsmarting your opponents. To accomplish this, you must learn to strategize. Eventually, you'll get to know the opposing players better, and you can develop strategies to exploit their weaknesses. In this section, we'll give you some tips and examples to get you started.

Offensive Strategies

There are lots of offensive strategies out there that can give your team an edge. Your coach probably knows a bunch already, but while you're learning those, you can also watch games on TV. See if you can pick out strategies and put them to good use—you'll be amazed at what you can learn.

For now, take a look at these three offensive strategies—with practice, they can be effective, giving your team a tactical edge.

Delayed Steals

Say you're at a base, and the baseman is keeping an eye on you. They're likely expecting you to make a run for it as soon as the pitcher releases that ball.

The solution? Don't.

Wait until the ball crosses home plate, then make a run for it. By switching it up with delayed steals, you can keep your opponents guessing. This simple offensive strategy can get you a lot of bases if you're fast and sneaky enough!

A Bunt for the Team

When you've got runners at the bases, one offensive strategy that can get you runs is having the batter "take a bunt for the team," also known as a sacrifice bunt. Instead of trying to knock the ball out of the park, the batter should tap the ball to the infield, directing focus to first base.

This lets the runners make their move, benefitting the entire team and is an excellent strategy for close, low-scoring games. It's best used with a weaker batter, so don't use this tactic when your best hitter is at bat.

Hitting for Steals

A batter can also make it easier for teammates to steal a base successfully by hitting the ball in the opposite direction, just far enough behind the runner to give a good head start.

For example, if you had a player at second base, the batter would hit the ball toward the right side of the infield. With a little luck, during the fielder's scramble, the player at second will have enough of a head start to make it easily to third.

DEFENSIVE STRATEGIES

A team's defense is pretty much headed by the pitcher, and the throws they prefer will determine where the ball is most likely to go. For instance, if your pitcher likes to throw pitches that dip down before they cross home plate, then you're going to be dealing with a lot of grounders, so be prepared. If fielders know in advance whether their pitcher will throw to the inside or the outside, they can shift accordingly, which gives them an edge for catching the ball.

One good idea is to create "part-time jobs" for every position. While each player has their assigned area to cover, each one can also be assigned as a backup for a teammate. This strengthens your defense and can help avoid confusion when a batter knocks a wild ball into the outfield.

For example, when a catcher isn't busy guarding home plate, they can help the first baseman from time to time. Similarly, when a ball goes to third base, the shortstop should be ready to assist if needed.

Remember, assigned positions are just your basic defense—think of them as a foundation to build on, and practice backing each other up. Your defense will be a lot tougher to crack if you work together.

Reading the Game and Making Quick Decisions

Practice makes perfect, as they say, but we have a few pointers on learning to read the game and making lightning-fast decisions that will help you win it! Keep these tips in mind:

Develop Game Awareness: When you aren't watching the ball, get in the habit of observing the other team—and your own—and keep up with the game stats. If you know where every player is and enough about each one's strengths and weaknesses, you can make fast, winning decisions at the best possible times.

Practice to Game Speed: You can slow down practice on a lazy day every now and again, but most practice games should take place at full game speed. That way, when you face an opponent, you'll be used to the faster pace, and it's just a matter of keeping cool under pressure.

Study Pitch Grips and Releases: Studying the grips for different pitches can give a keen-eyed batter an incredible edge. When your whole team makes an effort to learn and compare notes, you'll start noticing patterns that reveal the opposing pitcher's preferred throws. Watch videos and observe your own pitcher in the meantime, and though it takes a while, this time will be well-spent.

Good form Should be Automatic: Practice proper form for every position until it becomes automatic. Once you start using proper form without having to think about it, you'll play better and be able to focus your full attention on the game.

Decide Before You Catch: Fielders should plan where to send the ball before they catch it—not after. If you catch the ball and then look around to decide, you're just wasting time. Get in the habit of planning where you'll throw the ball while it's still in the air, and you'll be a better fielder for it.

COMMUNICATION AND TEAMWORK

With everyone taking responsibility for their own position and backing up another player, the other team will have a much harder time getting past your defense. Teamwork wins games, so you need to be able to communicate effectively on the field if you want to pull off those strategies you've practiced.

To do this, you need a combination of verbal and non-verbal communication, and you should always use it on the field—especially in practice.

Whether or not to use verbal communication depends on the distance between the two players, though you can and should switch things up from time to time, saying one thing with your mouth while a hand gesture communicates a secret play.

For the basics, however, use your proximity to teammates to get started. For instance, if the shortstop speaks softly, the third baseman will probably hear, and they should communicate with every pitch to stay coordinated.

However, the shortstop also needs to coordinate with the second baseman, but because of the distance, their communication will be non-verbal. This could be as easy as making faces behind your glove—the second baseman might smile to indicate they can cover their base or raise their eyebrows if they need backup from the shortstop.

Thinking about the distance between the teammates you need to communicate with makes it easy to choose whether to use verbal or non-verbal communication. Once you've got the hang of it, start sneaking in gestures. Before you know it, you'll be communicating secret strategies like the pros.

HANDLING HIGH-PRESSURE SITUATIONS

Playing live is stressful—people are watching, after all, and everyone is terrified of disappointing their teammates. That's why you should prepare yourself for the pressure of the game.

This starts with the whole team. Learn each other's strengths and weaknesses, but don't be hard on each other. While friends tease each other all the time, if you make another player feel insecure, they'll remember what you said and might choke up during a game.

The solution is simple: Don't tear others down—build each other up! Everyone has weak spots, and if you plan practices around improving these, you'll see a huge difference in everyone's skill and confidence.

You'll still have to deal with pressure, of course, but we have some strategies that can help with the stress of the game and spectators:

Hyperfocus: Instead of worrying about how people see you, focus on noticing as many details about the game as you can. Is your pitcher favoring fastballs today? How many outs are there right now? How many fly balls have been hit so far? Give your brain something useful to focus on, and your fears will melt away while your game awareness expands.

Breathing Exercises: A simple breathing exercise like a 5-2-5 can help you relax and get your focus back on the game. Breathe in from the stomach and diaphragm for five seconds, hold it for two, and breathe out for another count of five. This takes practice, but if you do it enough, it'll become automatic. Breathing helps you relax, and that extra oxygen boost will keep your mind sharp.

Keeping Busy: A little movement is good for you—it gets blood to your muscles so you're ready for explosive action when it's needed. If you're nervous, the worst thing to do is freeze, so shuffle and move your body a little to keep busy and get your focus back on the game.

DEVELOPING A GAME PLAN

If you're just getting started with baseball, you might not like your coach very much at first. After all, they keep assigning you exercises and telling you what to do. However, as much as you resent it right now, it's exactly what you need.

You're going to have to learn to trust your coach.

Developing a game plan with your coach ensures that you learn strategy to go with the new skills you're training, and it makes a huge difference—enough to win you the game.

Experienced coaches know great strategies and can provide helpful input—like using those scouting reports we mentioned, for instance, or by simply assessing your skills and giving you pointers on the spot.

The problem is that some strategies require that you've been putting in enough practice to use them—so the next time the coach asks you to do a drill that you don't like, just do it. Your coach knows what they're doing, and if you work together, everybody wins!

CHAPTER TEN: PRACTICING AND IMPROVING

We cannot stress the importance of practice enough. Baseball has a lot of moving parts, meaning that you need to develop a lot of skills in order to be a well-rounded player—and, thus, an asset to your team.

In this chapter, we're going to help you set your own improvement goals and create a practice schedule to work on your weaknesses and strengths. We'll also cover why mistakes are actually a good thing and finish up with some tips to keep yourself motivated through the process of becoming the best baseball player you can be.

SETTING GOALS FOR IMPROVEMENT

The first thing you need to do if you want to improve your baseball skills is set a few goals for yourself. The easiest way to do this is to buy a blank book from your local bookstore or, even better, a yearly planner.

A planner will have dates pre-written or blank spaces so you can write your own in, so you can write in your practice schedule, and even mark off completed practices. You can use a marker, for instance, to cross an X over completed training sessions, with a different color for games. This will help you to track the time you put in, as well as how many games you've played.

Ultimately, this allows you to track your goals. Planners usually have some space in the front for notes, and this is where you can write down your baseball goals. While you might be thinking to yourself, "I already know my goals!" writing them down helps you really commit to them.

Be realistic about the goals you set so you don't get discouraged. Setting too many gives you too much to work on—and you might even injure yourself trying to do too much—so start off by picking two positions that you want to work on and one specific skill in particular.

For instance, you might write, "I want to be a better pitcher and a better shortstop, and to improve my batting skills." Writing your goals down solidifies your commitment and allows you to personalize your training. Start off by looking at the required skills in Chapter 8 and use these as a guide.

For instance, if your goals are to be a better pitcher and shortstop, set your goals for these specific skills:

> **Pitcher:** Pitchers need to focus on throwing strength and accuracy, overall body strength, overall stamina, and resistance to pressure.
>
> **Shortstop:** Shortstops need to hone their agility and reflexes, along with throwing strength and accuracy, catching ability, field awareness, and overall game awareness.

Once you've identified the skills you need, go through and evaluate your current ability, then pick one skill that you need extra practice with. For example, both pitchers and shortstops need throwing strength and accuracy, but say you can throw the ball pretty far, but it doesn't always go where you want. That means you have the strength, so you'll need to work extra hard on your accuracy.

As you can see, there's plenty to use here for setting your goals! If you need more training than you get during practice, you can go to a batting cage at your local sports center once a week, for instance, to pursue your personal goal of working on your swing.

Now that you've got a starting point, you're probably wondering how you'll find time to do everything but relax—we've got you covered. Let's talk about how to create a practice schedule and stick to it.

CREATING A PRACTICE SCHEDULE

The most important thing to remember when setting a practice schedule is to make sure you can keep it. We recommend practicing three times a week for 1 ½ hours.

An hour and a half is doable, and it's plenty of time for several different drills between your warm-up and wind-down routines. Practicing three times a week also keeps your skills fresh and baseball on your mind, which is critical to help you stick with the game.

When you play games, you can count a game as a practice session to keep yourself from overdoing it.

If you're using a planner, creating your schedule is easy. Go for every other day—Tuesday, Thursday, and Saturday are usually perfect—and mark them in your planner. Otherwise, you can create a practice sheet and make copies for your teammates to make sure everyone will be there.

Practice is most effective when you divide it up into three categories: throwing drills, defensive drills, and batting practice. This allows you to build a foundation, and you can introduce different drills later when everyone is ready.

If you want to sneak in some personal training with a friend or on your own, that's fine, but don't work out the same muscles that you're using in practice—that's a surefire way to hurt yourself.

When you feel like your team is ready, take advantage of your local sports or recreation center if you can. Membership is usually inexpensive, and teams can also book time there occasionally, even without a membership, to take advantage of their training equipment. Switching things up is fun sometimes, and it helps build skill and confidence quickly, so be sure to look for these centers—they can help you take your training to the next level.

PLAYING TO YOUR STRENGTHS AND WEAKNESSES

Every player has strengths and weaknesses, and that's completely normal. No one is good at everything from the get-go. However, you do need to be honest with yourself about what you need to improve.

You should also be humble about the things you're already good at and practice these skills as well. After all, you've got some natural talent—why shouldn't you take advantage of it and see just how good you can be?

The easiest way to approach training is to break it down like this:

- Make regular, honest assessments of your skills.
- Plan drills to maintain and improve.
- Consider a regular exercise regimen.
- Make honest assessments of your skills regularly.

If you don't track your progress, how will you know if you're getting better? While you might think your game is improving, there's always a danger that pride is getting in the way, so the first aspect of your improvement program needs to be recording your stats.

There are a lot of things to track in baseball. For instance, you'll certainly be tracking batting averages and stolen bases. Especially in Little League, you'll keep count of pitches to make sure each pitcher stays within their limit to prevent injury.

Instead of making your own sheet from scratch, do a quick internet search to find free online templates. Remember when we talked about scouting reports in Chapter 7? When it comes to tracking your skills, this is the absolute best way to go. Use the keywords youth baseball scout report template, and you'll find lots of options to pick from, which you can then download and print. If someone on your team has experience using computers for layout/graphic design, you can even add the team logo to the template and make changes if you like.

When you log each practice and game, you'll have a reliable record of your progress. Just make sure your coach fills it out or, if you're just playing with friends, pair up to rate and record each other. This keeps things honest since you might be tempted to exaggerate your skills if you fill it out yourself, and that won't help you at all.

Drill for These Skills

Numbers don't lie, and they'll help you identify your weak spots and gauge improvement in these and the skills you're already strong in. In turn, this helps you set your personal training goals. Your coach can also use these numbers to choose training drills that benefit the whole team.

Another perk of scouting reports is that players who score high in areas where others need training can help teach that particular skill. Teaching is one of the best ways to improve—for both the student and the teacher—and having players tutor each other builds friendships and trust, resulting in a stronger bond between teammates.

CREATE AN EXERCISE ROUTINE

Sometimes, a player can have perfect form, but certain skills just don't seem to work the way they expect them to. The solution is almost always regular exercise. Remember, baseball is a sport, requiring stamina and muscle to power up developing skills and put them to good use. Exercising for just 20 minutes twice a week on your own can change your game dramatically.

Don't believe us? Fair enough—here's a challenge: Perform 20-minute exercise sessions twice a week for one month and see what happens. Target the specific muscles used for your position, and keep your routine low-impact—basically, take it easy with exercises that don't put a lot of strain on your muscles and joints.

To start with, try doing three sets of ten for each of these exercises:

- Push-ups
- Jumping Jacks
- Squat thrusts

In case you aren't familiar with that last one, here's how to do a squat thrust: Stand with your feet shoulder-width apart, arms at your sides. Next, squat and put your hands on the floor (also shoulder-width apart), then kick back into a push-up position. Reverse, return to the starting position, and repeat.

In addition to these, get some running in—say, three laps at your local public track or a trail in a nearby park—and you've got a great starting fitness routine that will benefit your game in the form of better control and more power.

TURN MISTAKES INTO LESSONS

Don't be discouraged when you make a mistake—everyone makes mistakes, so there's nothing to be ashamed of. More importantly, mistakes are actually a good thing, because each serves as a learning opportunity.

It's hard to be honest with ourselves about our shortcomings, and when we make a mistake, our first reaction is usually embarrassment. However, if you let it ruin your day, you're doing yourself a disservice.

Stay humble, and when you slip up, just ask yourself, "What could I have done better?" If it's something you can practice, then great—you've just found a way to improve your game. If it's something you can't practice or change, that's fine, too—it just means it was a fluke. Why be embarrassed over something you can't control?

Remember, every mistake is a gift, an honest and direct lesson on how you can improve your game. If you can develop this attitude and stick with it, the sky's the limit!

TIPS FOR STAYING MOTIVATED

While you're training, it's easy to get frustrated. When that happens, you might forget the most important thing—baseball is fun, and you're doing this because you love the game.

Everyone needs a little morale boost every now and again, so here are some tips to help stay motivated and on track:

> **Get to Know Your Teammates:** Everyone needs to know their teammates, so be sure to hang out between practices and get to know each other. A close team plays better together—it's as simple as that.
>
> **Don't Criticize, Do Instruct:** When you're practicing together, never criticize your teammates, and don't compare them to other players—unless you can do it constructively. For instance, saying something like "Why can't you catch the ball like John?" will only discourage your teammate. However, if you say, "Have you noticed how John holds his glove up this way right before he nails a catch? We can practice that if you want to. With your reach, I think you could make some great catches with the

same technique!" Instruct, don't criticize, and the whole team will benefit.

Post-Practice Praise: Get in the habit of a little post-practice praise. At the end of practice, compliment your teammates so they know they're getting better. Saying things like "Great pitches today!" or "Your batting form is perfect, how did you get that good?" motivates your fellow players, and you might even get useful tips or compliments of your own. Everyone likes positive feedback, so get in the habit of post-practice praising, and you'll see a difference quickly.

Practice Prizes: Talk with your coach about practice prizes as a motivator—either weekly, biweekly, or monthly. Parents may be asked to chip in anywhere from $1-$5 each, or you can even ask a local sports shop if they want to help support your team. Sometimes, businesses—especially smaller ones—are happy to provide modest pieces of gear to help promote their store and support their local team at the same time.

Always Back Up Your Teammates: When it's just you and your teammates, you probably give each other a little sass (okay, you definitely do, but hopefully everyone knows it's all in good fun). If someone else talks bad about a teammate, however, it's important to have each other's backs. Baseball is about sports, fun, and friendship—if everyone knows that their teammates support them, you'll be amazed at how much of a difference it makes, both at practice and in-game.

Don't Forget to Mark Your Training Planner: As you continue to practice and play games, don't forget to mark your training planner. It might seem silly at first but fill in that planner with markers or stickers and you'll be able to see your progress. This is one of the best ways to stay motivated.

CHAPTER ELEVEN: MENTAL TOUGHNESS

If you've ever mowed your lawn or done some summer work to earn a little extra cash, you know that hard work sometimes gives you blisters. Those blisters hurt, but eventually, they form calluses, and this tough skin lets you work even harder.

To get really good at baseball, you'll need to do the same thing, but with your mind. Like anything worthwhile in life, you'll need a battle plan—so in this chapter, we're going to build one.

While toughening up your mind might seem tricky, the key to tackling it is the same as any other job: Break it down into smaller, more manageable tasks. In this case, we'll turn the big, vague job of building mental toughness into two more targeted and realistic ones:

- Practice mental toughness techniques to deal with stress
- Develop a growth mindset to learn and stay motivated

If you're ready, let's break these down into even smaller goals, and by the end of this chapter, your baseball toughness battle plan will be laid out and ready for you to work it.

TECHNIQUES FOR PERFORMANCE ANXIETY

While your coach and some of your more experienced teammates might seem to have tough skin, every one of them had to build that resilience over time. Baseball can be stressful, after all, especially in the beginning.

When you're at bat, you've got a hard, fast-moving ball flying your way, and it's only natural to worry that it might hit you. As a baseman, you'll be worried about someone stealing a base or a teammate fumbling a catch. Fielders must dash after flyballs, running with their eyes to the sky, often without knowing if they're about to run into something.

Then, there are the fans — when you play live games, friends and family are watching, and baseball is famous for having a very vocal crowd, which can get under your skin if you let it.

First things first: Relax.

Feeling stressed about the game and about your personal performance is only natural. We all want to impress our friends, family, and any other spectators that might be watching. When you're first getting started, it can be overwhelming, but there are a few time-tested tricks that can help you get your Zen back and keep your head in the game.

Handling pressure and stress: Good habits to keep you consistently calm and cool

Before we go into relaxation techniques, we'll share some advice for keeping your cool in the game to help you develop good habits in stressful situations:

> **Breathe Before You Speak:** Always stop to take a deep breath to decide if you really need to say something. It doesn't seem like much but forcing yourself to pause for a moment can give you a clarity of thought that will make a big difference in what you say — or don't say — next.
>
> **Don't Escalate:** You're here to play. You don't make the rules, and you don't have the right to defy or enforce them yourself. If you argue and make things worse, you won't help yourself or your team when you get kicked out of the game.
>
> **Don't Be a Fish:** When someone tries to rile you up, don't take the bait. They're trying to psych you out, and if you let them make you angry, it will affect your game. Taking the bait is your choice — don't give them that kind of power over you.
>
> **Mediation Instead of Confrontation:** Why waste time arguing? Tell the other person "Let's let someone neutral

make the call, and I'll agree to follow it," and ask an umpire or team captain—anyone neutral will do—to decide who's right, then and there. Keep your word and let it be settled. If you don't like the call, playing better is the best revenge.

The Rules are the Rules: Get in the habit of accepting the rules. They're there for a reason, and nobody gets a special exception.

Remember that Your Teammates are Watching: If you want to be a leader, lead by example. You might not feel calm but do your best to "fake it till you make it." Your teammates are watching, and if you can do it, they'll try harder. Imagine the power of an entire team that always keeps its cool!

Sometimes, the pressure of the game gets to you, even with your usual tricks, so it's good to have backup techniques to help keep you calm. Here are a few ways to relax and get your focus back on the game:

Keep Moving: If you can move a little in the position you're playing, do it. Go over inning stats in your mind, moving your focus into the game. Sometimes all it takes is a little extra movement to channel that agitation somewhere useful.

Breathing Exercises: In chapter 9, we shared the 5-2-5 breathing exercise. One variation of this is the 3-3-3: Breathe in for a count of three, hold it for a count of three, and exhale for a count of three. That extra oxygen will help you relax, and if you practice this or the 5-2-5, it will become automatic later when you start to get anxious.

Channel Your Idol: Everyone has a favorite baseball player, so imagine yourself as that person. Ask yourself what they would do in your place and go with it—a little inspiration goes a long way!

Visualization and Mental Rehearsal

Another great way to defeat performance anxiety is to get aggressive with your stress. Visualize your next move and rehearse it in your mind. Are you going to throw a certain pitch? Are you going to bunt the ball? Go through the movements mentally so that when the moment arrives, you're 110% ready.

Getting in the habit of being one move ahead is tricky at first, but if you keep at it, you'll take your skills to the next level. Don't stress — instead, use that nervous energy to think ahead. The other players won't know what hit them!

Developing a Growth Mindset

In addition to dealing with performance stress and other people, you also need to develop a growth mindset if you want to become a better player. Basically, this means establishing confidence in your growing skills and teaching yourself to view mistakes as learning opportunities.

Nobody Starts Out Perfect

It's your mind, so you're the boss—and coincidentally, the acronym BOSS has a plan built right into it:

> **Build up Confidence and Self-Belief:** You've got the will; you've just got to build the skill—and don't you forget it! You've made the commitment to play, and if you keep learning, opposing teams will start dreading it whenever you step up to the plate or the mound. Think about that when you're discouraged because you can make that happen if you keep pushing.

> **Overcome Mistakes and Setbacks by Learning from Them:** Don't punish yourself for mistakes—learn from them. When someone criticizes you, if they're right, they're doing you a favor by telling you what you need to learn. If you can adopt this attitude, the sky's the limit!

Stay Positive and Motivated: You're going to win, or you're going to learn. Either way, you're playing a game you love. Keep that in mind, and smile while you think about it—smiles are infectious, and that attitude can take you to the top.

Stick with Your Practice: Skill takes time to develop, and there are no shortcuts. If you want to get better, you've got to do those practice drills, exercise your body, and toughen up your mind. Work with your coach and keep a log of your stats to motivate yourself. We guarantee they'll go up over time if you stick with it.

CHAPTER TWELVE: PLAYING WITH RESPECT AND SPORTSMANSHIP

Baseball will teach you many skills that apply to the rest of your life. Two of the most important ones are respect and good sportsmanship. Baseball has a framework of rules, and to win, you have to cooperate with your teammates and the people making the tough calls during games.

You can't do this without proper respect. For instance, if you don't respect your teammates, do you think they're going to have your back? Will they respect you? Odds are, they won't. If your team doesn't get along, you're already putting yourselves at a disadvantage.

If you don't respect a teammate's skills, do yourself a favor and show them respect for their courage to stick with it and for your shared love of the game. Give a little respect and a chance to earn more— you're all in this together, after all.

Umpires and coaches deserve respect as well. Umpires have a hard time of things, making difficult calls that don't exactly make them popular—but you know what? They do it to keep the game fair for everyone. You might not always agree with them, but ask yourself this: Would you like to be the one getting yelled at in every game? You know you probably wouldn't, so show a little respect. If anyone loves the game, it's an umpire, because nobody would take so much trash talk just for the fun of it!

Coaches also deserve your respect, even if you feel like they're drilling you to death in practice or if you don't like their ideas. Your coach sees the bigger picture of the game, and while you'll learn to do this eventually, the bottom line is that your coach knows every team member's strengths and weaknesses. What's more, they've probably studied your opponents.

Ever see your coach argue with the umpire? If so, they're probably doing it for you. Many coaches have been kicked out of a game, and you might have thought it was for their temper—but it wasn't. Your coach didn't like the call, and they had your back.

Show some respect when your coach is drilling you over and over in a particular skill, and put 110% into practicing it. Keeping you motivated and helping you improve are two of a coaches' many jobs, but they sometimes focus on the "play better" part and let you handle the motivation on your own.

Don't take it personally, though. Your progress will make them proud, and in the future, you might get to enjoy hearing them jawing at the umpire for you!

HANDLING WINS AND LOSSES GRACEFULLY

Once you've learned respect, good sportsmanship comes easily. When you win, don't be a jerk about it—you and your teammates have practiced hard, and the opposing team gave you a chance to show off your hard work. Thank them for it by being a gracious winner.

The same goes for losing. Losing isn't fun, but you've gained something from it: insight into what you need to work on. Thank your opponents for a good game, and when the team gets together afterward, talk with your teammates and coach to decide the best drills to prepare for playing that team next time.

When you think about it like that, either way, you're getting something good. You either experience the pride and glory of a victory, or you gain valuable lessons you couldn't get anywhere else—unless, of course, you spend your time sulking or blaming others and leave those valuable lessons laying on the diamond, unlearned.

The choice is yours!

BUILDING TEAM SPIRIT

We've talked about respecting your teammates, but you're also responsible for building each other up. If someone on your team isn't confident about a skill, and it's something you're good at, offer to practice with them. When you do, mention something they do well—everyone loves compliments—and besides, they might be able to teach you a thing or two.

When you build each other up and hang out after games, it's only natural that you'll develop team spirit, and that's a great thing. Every player is unique, so every team is also unique. Embrace the attitude that you team is special, and build each other up. If you work together, you'll be a force to be reckoned with—and the other teams will know it.

LIFELONG BENEFITS OF PLAYING WITH INTEGRITY

We've mentioned that respect and good sportsmanship will take you far and that you'll be able to apply these skills throughout the rest of your life—so what does that really mean?

To put it simply, life is like baseball in a lot of important ways. For one thing, just like those countless drills make you a better player, a college education can make you better in whatever field you decide to study.

Treating others with respect is also a fundamental lesson. Whenever you give someone basic respect and the chance to earn more, they might well surprise you. One day, when you have a career, even if it's not pro baseball, respect still goes a long way. Your coworkers will notice it and show you respect in return, especially if you strive to be a role model like you do with your team.

Umpires make calls that you won't always like, and that's going to happen a lot in life, too. Rules are everywhere, and if you learn them—and learn from them—instead of letting them get you down, you'll find ways to succeed, just like you did in baseball.

Most importantly, by being a good sport in life like you've learned to be in baseball, you'll master one of the most valuable lessons of all: There's always a new game, and this time, you'll be prepared. Who knows? You might just win!

CHAPTER THIRTEEN: BEYOND THE BASICS

Now that you've reached this final chapter, you're probably wondering, "What about when I'm ready for advanced techniques?" Well, we've put together some tips—and more importantly, we'll share some free resources you can take advantage of to advance your skills on your own.

After that, we'll relate a few stories from baseball greats before we wrap things up properly so you can start taking advantage of what you've learned in this book.

With that said, let's get started on those tips, and we'll go from there.

UPGRADING YOUR PASSING THROW

One common mistake players make when throwing long-distance passes from the outfield is a tendency to treat it like a regular pitch, holding the ball low at the hip so it circles around to get enough power.

While that works, it's slow—and worse, it's not very accurate. There's a better way to do it. Get in the habit of throwing your long-distance passes from the outfield like this:

1. With your side facing your target, hold the ball up a little above your shoulder. Point your elbow straight down, and bring your other hand up, just in front of the ball.
2. Take a step toward your target and throw the ball across your body, twisting so your chest is facing the target before you release the ball.

Over time, your arms will strengthen with this simple technique, and you'll be surprised just how far you can pass the ball.

ADVANCED HITTING TIP

Advanced hitting tip: Start looking right down the middle of the plate

Since a pitch is usually aimed toward the outside, many batters keep their eyes on the outer portion of the plate, but another simple but effective strategy is to focus your attention straight down the middle of the plate.

This gives you the best view for the pitches you can hit the hardest. If the pitcher does throw the ball to the outside of the plate, that's fine—you can quickly adjust to hit it. Keeping your attention on the middle of the plate, however, gives you a better chance to take advantage of opportunities to knock the ball out of the park.

ADVANCED PITCHING

When it comes to pitching, the best advice we can give is to focus on your form. Lifting your leg, making that circle as you wind up—proper form gives you the power and accuracy that you need, provided that you do it right.

To practice form, you can invest in two cheap webcams and place one in front of you, and the other to the side. You can run two web cameras at the same time, but unless you have software designed to show multiple camera views at once, you'll have to settle for recording it with two different programs.

Alternatively, you can enlist a teammate who also wants to practice pitching and record each other with your phones. This will let you see your stance so you can work on it until it's perfect.

You should also practice the different grips we explained in Chapter 6, but you can find even more on the MLB website. Visit https://www.mlb.com/glossary/pitch-types to access a list of 14 pitches used in Major League games. Even better, there's a video for each one, so you can study the pitcher to help you to learn. If you're having trouble with a specific grip, search for the name of the pitch or grip on the internet for free information to teach yourself some of the sneakiest pitches around.

If the official MLB website ever goes down, don't worry—as long as you have perfect form, knowing the grip and proper way to release should be enough, so looking up "How to throw a" with the name of the pitch you're interested in will still give you everything you need—except for the practice, of course!

Some pitches are difficult to learn, and it could take years to master some of the trickiest throws. With that said, if you dream of pitching in the Major Leagues, it's time to start practicing. You can do this—it's all about putting in the work by practicing until those pitches are yours!

Speaking of online resources, there are quite a few that you can find on your own by searching for free baseball resources. Below, we've listed some of the best we found online (at the time of writing this book).

TIPS, EQUIPMENT, DRILLS, AND RESOURCES

Free Equipment

Several non-profit organizations work with youth baseball groups all over the United States to help provide quality equipment where it's needed. Here are three examples:

> **Leveling the Playing Field:**
> https://www.levelingtheplayingfield.org

Good Sports:
https://www.goodsports.org

Youth Development Foundation:
https://www.baseballydf.com

Free Coaching Drills

PCA Development Zone is a website produced by the Positive Coaching Alliance, a non-profit organization that provides free resources for coaches and partners with local communities to make sports a positive and equal-opportunity experience. They have a lot of useful information, a good example of which is a page for free coaching drills:

(https://devzone.positivecoach.org/resource/externallink/baseball-resources-and-drills-coaches).

Check it out and see what you think. It's not just good for coaches—players can also find some great information that they can use.

A Free Historical Baseball Treasure Trove

The Library of Congress provides an amazing, 100%-free archive of baseball history content you can access by visiting https://guides.loc.gov/baseball/online-library-resources or by searching for baseball resources at the Library of Congress.

There, you can find old books on baseball, historical scouting reports, and even neat things like baseball cards from the early 1900s! If you want to learn about the history of baseball, this site is a real gem, and you're going to love it.

Free Baseball Instruction from Pros

Pro Baseball Insider is a website with a lot of free resources available, including free instruction videos from pro Baseball players to up your game. You can check those out by visiting https://probaseballinsider.com or by searching for "Pro Baseball Insider free baseball instruction."

STORIES AND TIPS FROM PRO PLAYERS

We all need a little inspiration sometimes, so in this section, we'll share three stories about professional players who beat the odds and got to the top, along with some tips toward the end of the section.

Mordecai Peter Centennial Brown

Mordecai Brown is a baseball legend whose 14-year career led him to pitch for five different teams: The Cincinnati Reds, Chicago Cubs, Chicago Whales, Saint Louis Terriers, and Brooklyn Tip-Tops. What's so special about that, you might ask?

He did it with only three fingers on his right hand.

When Mordecai was a kid, he lost two fingers in a farming accident, ending up stuck with the nickname "Three Finger Brown."

Growing up, Mordecai loved baseball, and he even played in the semi-pros for a while. Then, he discovered something that made him switch from the infield to the mound and helped him earn a career in the pros—Mordecai found that those missing parts of his fingers allowed him to throw an evil curveball!

The rest, as they say, is history—but if you need a little reminder that love of the game and determination are a winning combination against all odds, then be sure to think about Mordecai—he wanted to play, and by golly, he did it his way!

Ryne Duren

If you're worried don't have the eagle eyes needed to be a good pitcher, think again—Ryne Duren was a player for the St. Louis Browns who had 20/200 vision in his left eye and 20/70 vision in his right. Simply put, he was legally blind in one eye and could barely see in the other!

That didn't stop him from playing, though. While it must be pretty scary at bat when you can barely see, Ryne earned his glory on the pitching mound. Sporting Coke bottle glasses with red lenses, he made the news for throwing a 100-mile-per-hour fastball in front of an amazed crowd.

Ryne's fastball made him one of the best relief pitchers in Major League Baseball between 1958 and 1959 and even earned him four All-Star appearances with the New York Yankees.

While his stats were modest, he was one of the hardest throwers in baseball in his day, and despite being "blind as a bat," he commanded the respect of both his teammates and other teams for the duration of his impressive 10-year career.

Just something to think about if you're worried that your eyesight isn't great—Ryne's wasn't, and it sure didn't stop him!

Cal Ripken

You know how we said you shouldn't skip out on practice? One baseball pro you may have heard of, Cal Ripken, obviously took that lesson to heart—and you know what? It got him far.

From 1981 to 2001, Cal made sure to put in his practice and be there for his team for the entirety of his 21-season career with the Baltimore Orioles, so much that he holds the record for the most consecutive baseball games played—a whopping 2,632!

All that practice definitely paid off—Cal is in the record books as one of only ten players in baseball history to achieve 400 home runs and 3000 hits. Next time you feel like skipping practice, think about Cal—he didn't, and neither should you!

CONCLUSION

We hope that you've enjoyed Baseball Skills for Kids. Before we go, we want to share some encouragement to help you on your journey of learning America's favorite pastime. While there's a lot to learn, we want you to remember the most important aspect of the game: Have fun! Baseball is a wonderful game that will teach you good sportsmanship and how to work as a team, and it's also going to give you amazing stories you'll treasure for the rest of your life.

Whether you have dreams of going pro or simply love playing the game and spending time with your friends, the tips and tricks we've shared here will help you get stronger and better, so you'll be able to enjoy baseball even more.

Remember that every win is a reward for your hard work, not an excuse to trash-talk the other team. On the flip side, when it's your team that loses, remember that the other team has given you a gift by showing you exactly how to make your team better.

Finally, our last piece of advice is that you've got to practice. Be there for every drill and game when you can, just like Cal Ripken. Baseball requires a lot of commitment in the form of practice and the attention you'll need to learn all the secrets of the game.

If you're up to the task, the rewards will last a lifetime—and who knows? Someday, you may be teaching your own kids how to play your favorite game!

Thanks so much for reading, and now that we've said a proper goodbye, what are you waiting for? You've got some baseball skills to practice! Maybe someday, if you work hard enough, they'll take you all the way to the pros!

www.ingramcontent.com/pod-product-compliance
Lightning Source LLC
Chambersburg PA
CBHW070108080526
44586CB00013B/1230